School

Public Libraries

Developing
the Natural
Alliance

Natalie Reif Ziarnik

American Library Association
Chicago
2003

While extensive effort has gone into ensuring the reliability of information appearing in this book, the publisher makes no warranty, express or implied, on the accuracy or reliability of the information, and does not assume and hereby disclaims any liability to any person for any loss or damage caused by errors or omissions in this publication.

Composition by ALA Editions in Myriad Roman and Galliard using Quark XPress 4.1 on a PC Platform

Printed on 50-pound white offset, a pH-neutral stock, and bound in 10-point coated cover stock by Victor Graphics

The paper used in this publication meets the minimum requirements of American National Standard for Information Sciences—Permanence of Paper for Printed Library Materials, ANSI Z39.48-1992. ∞

Library of Congress Cataloging-in-Publication Data

Ziarnik, Natalie Reif.
    School and public libraries : developing the natural alliance/ by Natalie Reif Ziarnik.
       p. cm.
    Includes bibliographical references and index.
    ISBN 0-8389-0841-1
    1. Libraries and schools—United States. 2. Libraries and students—United States. I. Title.
    Z718 .Z53 2002
    027.4'0973—dc21   2002008971

Printed in the United States of America

07 06 05 04 03   5 4 3 2 1

Contents

Acknowledgments

As this book hopes to illustrate, we work in a web of connections. I am grateful to the following individuals who contributed to the creation of this book:

Renée Vaillancourt, for strongly suggesting I get back to writing and offering feedback during the early stages of this book; Brenda Duff, for hiring me as a school liaison and providing excellent guidance along the way; Barb Kalchbrenner, for nagging me kindly; Pam Allen, for laughing with me when needed; Rachel Davis and Erica Christianson, for showing me, over and over, that simple is better; Dawn Scarbeck and Kay Chisamore, for chocolate and encouragement; Bridget Hennessey and John Bailie, for showing me the importance of friendship; Kathleen Flatow, for inspiring discipline and focus at work; and to all the other staff at the Ela Area Public Library District who encouraged me and endured my absentmindedness while I was writing this book.

I also wish to thank the North Suburban Library System (NSLS) School Facilitators' Group. If it hadn't been for our meetings, I would not have felt compelled to begin this project. Judy Salganik and Margaret Poska, members of that group, kindly gave me permission to include descriptions of their programs in this book. Other faithful members gave their time to fill out surveys and stay late after meetings to talk with me about issues related to school-public library relations.

Interviews with the staff at other libraries offered new insights. I send my thanks to Jill Rodriguez and Penny Mandziara at the Bensenville Community Public Library, Bensenville, Illinois; Amy Gee at the Carthage

Public Library, Carthage, Illinois; and Amanda Hovious at the Palatine Public Library, Palatine, Illinois.

I am especially grateful to Amy Brandt, mostly for her friendship but also for meeting me at Lake Geneva for in-depth discussions of this book; Kathleen Lovelace, for her critiques and encouragement during this process and for her contribution to the chapter on grants; Betsy Hearne, for helping me find my professional calling; and Christine Jenkins, for her earlier warm welcome to the profession as well as her help on this project, including source suggestions, advice on my history chapter, and tips on archival research.

Most of all, I thank my husband, Andy, and my son, Zachary, for their patience, love, and flexibility during the writing of this book.

Introduction

Every other month, I attend the school facilitators' meeting at the North Suburban Library System (NSLS) headquarters in Wheeling, Illinois. At those meetings, public librarians discuss common concerns and ideas for fostering good relationships with schools. Often the sessions are helpful, even inspirational, but one meeting in September 2000 was an especially whiny one, and I left with the complaints of other librarians flooding my mind. I asked myself, "Why do they have so many problems? Why are they filled with bitterness? Why aren't they invited to the schools to give book talks? Why do their school librarians hate them?" Since I rarely encountered resistance at any of the schools I worked with, I felt both naive and confused.

I am fortunate that in Lake Zurich, Illinois, the public library where I work has, for the most part, a strong relationship with the schools. The nature of our relationship may be linked to the history of the library and the town's growth. In 1972, the public library began as an experimental project in a church basement. The parochial school connected to the church made excellent use of that library, and the library staff were happy to serve students and teachers, whether in the public library's space or in the school's classrooms. Over time the public library grew and moved out of the church basement into its own building, which was subsequently expanded only a few years later. Just this year, we moved into a new building over twice the size of our former one. As the library and community have grown, the library staff has continued its close relationship not only with the parochial school but also with other schools in the library's district. We have consistently followed the wise advice of Margaret A.

Edwards. In her book *The Fair Garden and the Swarm of Beasts* (1969), Edwards states that schools and public libraries "should work hand in glove to develop each student to his full potential as a reader." How, I wondered, could anyone think otherwise?

Comments at subsequent meetings at NSLS continued to haunt me and occupied more of my energy, especially after Renée Vaillancourt asked me to write a book proposal on the topic. Her request had sparked my curiosity; I found myself often asking the question *why* and began stumbling upon articles about school–public library relations. Underlying, yet unstated, tensions between public librarians, school librarians, and teachers jumped out at me from the articles' pages, and as I learned more, I acknowledged that this tense feeling was not just a product of my intuitive reaction style.

I ordered more and more articles on the history of librarianship and education. As I read the articles, I thought, "Oh, well, *that* explains it. If *that* happened, then of course librarians feel this way." The source of librarians' daily tensions was explained by events that took place many decades ago, yet the correlation seemed almost too simple. Since many of us are unfamiliar with our professions' histories, how do we account for the continued tension? How many librarians working today know that public librarians and school librarians had a huge falling-out in 1951? How many know the details of the Fairy Tale War, whose main players were Anne Carroll Moore, Lucy Sprague Mitchell, Margaret Wise Brown, and Frances Clarke Sayers?

Part of today's tension is newly created, arising out of current misunderstandings and lack of frequent communication. But that feeling of being different from one another has more power than we admit; it has been passed down from one generation of librarians to another. Even though the details of our professions' histories remain hazy, we have inherited a subtle apprehension and mistrust of others. This apprehension manifests itself when we hesitate to make contact with each other, overlook what our colleagues at other institutions are doing, or jump to false conclusions about each other. The history of our past lives with us daily.

I hope the history of our predecessors presented in chapter 1 will help explain and clear some of the tensions that prevent school and public librarians and teachers from working together as much as they could. The chapter is also filled with examples of a strong commitment to help youth by promoting reading and information literacy. That commitment continues to define us both professionally and personally.

The strengths of school and public libraries highlighted in the historical overview are examined in today's context in the remainder of the book. Chapter 2 outlines the different strengths of school and public libraries and shows how they provide complementary services in their communities to reach common goals. Chapters 3 through 7 function as a practical guide to lead you, step-by-step, to a more beneficial, cooperative working relationship with colleagues at the "other" institution, whether that be a school or public library. Many of the tips offered in those chapters were acquired through my experience as a school liaison. I have also included the insights and experiences of other public and school librarians interviewed for this book. Practical advice will address the following questions: How does one initiate contact with librarians at another institution? What are some strategies for gathering information about current and upcoming assignments? How can librarians improve their communication with teachers? How does one apply for grants? How do we convince teachers and students that the research process takes time?

These first six chapters were written with school and public librarians equally in mind, but chapter 7, "School Services at the Public Library," directly addresses the challenges and opportunities encountered in a public library setting, such as offering teachers special lending privileges or establishing a homework center.

The book then progresses from practical issues to personal approaches. In chapter 8, "A Day in the Life," I describe the rhythm and details of my workday, hoping to illustrate the constant interaction that takes place between public libraries and schools. Penny Mandziara, from the Bensenville Community Public Library, was kind enough to write about her typical day; she has a similar position to mine but emphasizes some other approaches to achieving the same overall goal of promoting school–public library cooperation. For contrast, Cynthia Oakes and Loretta M. Gaffney describe the typical day of a middle-school librarian at the University of Chicago Lab Schools. Please enjoy these glimpses of the joys and struggles experienced during another person's day at work.

The final chapter of the book, "At the Potter's Wheel," takes all the preceding material and throws it into action. It presents a collection of programming ideas that illustrate how to facilitate good school–public library interactions. Please feel free to adapt those ideas that spark your creativity and discard the rest. Each librarian approaches programming in such an individualized way that one librarian cannot hope to write an exact prescription for another.

While working on the last chapter, I talked with many other librarians, asking them to share programming ideas. Each individual who offered me an idea also recommended that I speak with two or three other people. I would have loved to include descriptions of all the programs I learned about, but time and space presented unwanted restrictions. All the people I talked with were so enthusiastic and proud of their work that my hope for excellent school–public library relations grew stronger daily. May this book strengthen your hope as well.

1 An Abbreviated History

THE PROGRESSIVE ERA (1890 TO 1920)

Whether you identify yourself as a public librarian, school teacher, teacher-librarian, school librarian, media specialist, or information specialist, the roots of your profession became strongly established between 1890 and 1920, a time known as the Progressive Era. The fields of education and librarianship, as well as the sister fields of nursing and social work, developed their core values and professional standards during this period of great social progress in the United States.

Members of these social welfare professions felt compelled to take action against the deplorable living conditions in American cities brought on by the economic depression of 1893. At the end of the nineteenth century, many people moved to cities. Rapid industrialization had created new factory and office jobs in the city for those who had lived in rural areas as well as for tens of thousands of recent immigrants. These new city inhabitants had to adjust to a different way of life. The working class was routinely subjected to dangerous working conditions and resided in unsanitary tenement buildings. Masses of children were uneducated and illiterate. Communicable diseases spread rampantly because the general population had no knowledge of basic germ theory and the importance of cleanliness. Those living in rural America had their own set of problems: the lack of good roads and postal service to these areas inhibited access to essential materials, including books and newspapers.

The middle class, especially educated middle-class women, were shocked at how miserable people's lives were and aimed to improve conditions through social reform and through their participation in the welfare professions—social work, teaching, librarianship, and nursing. The women entering and defining these professions were still strongly influenced by the Victorian ideology of the domestic "angel of the house" in which women stayed within the safe confines of home and shared their "superior moral insight" with their families. As the Victorian period began to wane, many women, especially those who did not marry, left their domestic, private spheres for a more public life, organizing with others in a zealous effort to improve society:

> No longer confined to the private sphere, they now used their legendary powers of moral suasion and their social consciences in the public domain. Breathing the hope and optimism of the age, confident in their own abilities, they marched into the first two decades of the twentieth century. (Schneider 1993)

In defining the helping professions and establishing professional associations and standards, these women pioneers fought against the notion that women were too weak or delicate to work outside the home. Yet, at the same time, they channeled their energy into areas often associated with their gender—educating, healing, and making a safe home for others. More and more middle-class women were graduating from college, where they were encouraged to contribute to society through work. In addition, since these women were usually unmarried, all of the love they would have directed toward a family was devoted to their work, which they saw as "social housekeeping."

All American teachers and librarians—whether male or female—share this common history and, as a consequence, common values that are just as strong today as they were one hundred years ago. The history of professions during the Progressive Era shows us how much public librarians, teachers, and school librarians (the latter being a combination of the two earlier established professions) have in common: all hoped and believed they could improve society through hard work, organization, and the education of the young.

The can-do spirit of the Progressive Era naturally flourished in the fields of education and librarianship; less obviously, however, this same spirit transformed the world of book publishing. As with the professions being in part a response to deplorable living and working conditions, the trends in publishing children's books responded to mass-market literature of poor literary and moral quality. Instead of criticizing and forbidding the reading of this literature, children's librarians and editors and writers of children's books took a more positive approach: they created excellent literature and encouraged young people to read it.

The critic Anne Lundin (1996) claims that the weaving together of the fields of education, librarianship, and publishing created a "peculiar synergy" that transformed the types of services and literature offered to children. Beginning in 1900, teachers and, especially, children's librarians exerted their influence on the publication of quality children's literature, creating what later became known as the Golden Age in American Children's Literature (1900 to 1950). Children's books modeled values "espoused by educated middle-class women . . . cooperation, friendship, acceptance, and tolerance on a personal, community, and international level" (Jenkins 1996). To promote the creation of books with these values, as well as with high literary quality and child appeal, children's librarians communicated their needs to writers and publishers and were often instrumental in the success and failure of juvenile titles.

Beginning in the Progressive Era and extending further into the twentieth century, librarians, teachers, writers, and publishers worked together to create and define excellent books and services for young people. The Golden Age of Children's Literature, initiated during this optimistic period, was one of the most significant products of this peculiar synergy. As we look back in history, there are other great moments of cooperation, particularly when the fields of education and librarianship join forces, either consciously or unconsciously. Our history was also influenced by people with strong personalities working in different environments, developing their own philosophies about library service and education for young people and spreading their influence by training future professionals.

TRACING THE STORY OF PUBLIC LIBRARY–SCHOOL RELATIONS

This section presents an overview of the contributions of the individuals who played major roles in the history of school–public library relations: Anne Carroll Moore, John Cotton Dana, Lutie Stearns, Mary Hall, Lucy

Sprague Mitchell, Margaret Wise Brown, Margaret Batchelder, and Frances Henne. By looking back at the professional lives of these individuals, one can see that the missions of schools and libraries definitely overlapped. There were times of great cooperation and joining of forces followed by times of separation and specialization again followed by times of renewed cooperation. This fluctuation can be seen as a natural process as times change and professions continually redefine themselves to meet new challenges. The pioneers of these professions tended to have strong opinions and greatly influenced the policies of the institutions in which they worked.

The Early Influences of Anne Carroll Moore (1900 to 1918)

Anne Carroll Moore, one of the foremothers of children's librarianship, worked in the midst of the peculiar synergy described earlier, using the strength of her powerful personality and convictions to define children's public library services and to set the standards for quality literature for young people. Moore was trained as a librarian at Pratt Institute and then began her career as a children's librarian at the Pratt Children's Library in Brooklyn, New York. The Pratt Institute was an institution of higher education for future librarians and artists as well as for those planning to enter a wide variety of vocational work. In her job at the library, Moore worked first and foremost to establish the area as a pleasant, hospitable place that children would want to visit voluntarily. Even though Moore viewed the work of a children's librarian as rooted in both education and social work, she insisted that the neighborhood library not resemble a school. This focus influenced her initial philosophy of school service. Moore (1902) was not prepared to send books to the schools or to supply "school duplicates." Instead, she wished to encourage the teachers and children to visit the neighborhood library, where librarians would "give them every possible means of assistance in connection with their school work as well as in their general reading."

To persuade teachers and their students to visit the library, Moore and her staff began a series of visits to the local Brooklyn public schools. The purpose of these visits was to publicize the library, to become familiar with the schools' environments, and to learn more about the reading ability of children in certain grades. Moore, who was not a big fan of schools in general, related incidents from these early difficult visits in her article "Visits to

Public Schools," published in *Library Journal* in April 1902: letters sent to principals received little notice, the librarian was rushed through a speedy tour of the school and was not allowed to speak to the classes, and public library activities of interest to school children were rarely promoted. Today one might wonder why Anne Carroll Moore had so many problems. Were the principal and teachers too busy to pay attention to the librarian? Was Moore's personality too assertive? Were the environments and culture of the public library and the schools too different from each other? Or had school curricula taken a step backwards, with no room for pleasure reading?

With experience, Moore and her staff developed a better awareness of schools' missions and curricula as well as an appreciation of the activities occurring during a typical school day. The Pratt Children's Library refined its philosophy of school service, taking the first steps toward what we today call school outreach. One defining moment occurred during a school visit when a librarian from Pratt was denied permission to speak about a current exhibit at the library during the school's opening exercises. With little hope of ever speaking with the school children, the librarian was beginning to leave the school when she heard music:

> Looking through the stairway window she saw an old man, with the sunniest smile, standing in the midst of a room full of happy-faced children and drawing his bow across his fiddle as if he loved it and could not help it.
>
> Presently they all began to sing, quite naturally and spontaneously. One felt at once, even through dingy glass, that the relations were absolutely harmonious between the children, the teacher, and the old violin player. (Moore 1902)

The old man's smile, his intimate connection to his art, and the natural and joyous manner in which he shared music with the children inspired the librarians at Pratt to take on a more interactive and personal approach to their school visits. The following techniques and goals were incorporated into the children's librarian's work:

- To show an obvious and natural love for their art/subject
- To fill the need for beauty in children's lives
- To aspire to have harmonious relationships with teachers and students

Anne Carroll Moore (1902) implored her staff "to so master the technique of [their] subject as to be able to present its essence as the violin player presented his melody." And, what is this "essence" of a children's librarian's "subject"? While contemplating this episode, Moore came to the following conclusions:

> Books must seem to us like real life, and human experience must seem like chapters from unwritten books.
>
> There is a certain technique of library visits to schools which seems to me to consist in taking things exactly as one finds them and adapting one's self so completely and cheerfully to the situation, whether it means sitting in an office, standing in a passage way, rushing through classrooms, receiving polite but immediate dismissal, or having pleasant talks with children and teachers, as to make it seem the most natural experience in the world while it lasts, and to make it the basis for future experiences. Theories, methods, the habit of looking too early for results, and above all, an aggressive or a too retiring personality, must be got rid of at any cost if we are to beget a love for books and win confidence and respect for our ways of giving them into the hands of those who want them, or who may be induced to want them.

Moore's language suggests that public librarians had to walk a fine line between actively promoting their services and vision and lying low and waiting for children and teachers to come to them spontaneously. In addition, the emphasis on "adapting one's self so completely and cheerfully," having "pleasant talks," and avoiding an "aggressive" personality may reflect Moore's attempts at caution while crossing the boundary that separated schools from libraries. By merging gradually with the daily rhythms of the school day, visiting public librarians hoped to cause fewer disruptions and encounter less resistance.

In an attempt to share the essence of their subject, Moore and her staff began incorporating storytelling and personal stories about books and libraries into their school visits. This change led to an emphasis on storytelling and book talks at the Pratt Children's Library and also helped the librarians further define how their role differed from the role of a teacher. The distinction between "telling things"—whether folktales or personal stories—and "teaching" was crucial, as Moore felt that children resented "particularly in the freedom of the library, any hint of being purposefully and systematically instructed" (Sayers 1972). Although the library had resources for students and teachers, in Moore's view, it should never come to resemble a school. Several years later, in 1914, when she was working at the New York Public Library (NYPL), Moore writes of this danger:

> There is a great danger of turning a children's library into a school grade extra by pushing of school work until library attendance ceases to be voluntary. On the day that everybody gets "sent" we lose the most valuable clause in our charter of liberty. (Moore quoted in Sayers 1972)

Moore's writings suggest that she did not see schools in a favorable light, although she was willing to acknowledge the expertise and talent of many teachers. Schools, in Moore's opinion, resembled prisons where teachers and administrators treated students like inmates. On a librarian's tour of one public school, she was rushed through the corridors at a breathless pace and wondered to herself, "How might one hope to penetrate walls of apparent impenetrability and really come to know the inmates?" The next day, a child accompanied by some classmates visited the librarian at Pratt and said "When I saw our principal *chase* you through our school yesterday I thought I'd like to belong [to the library] again" (Moore 1902).

For years, Anne Carroll Moore resisted sending library books to schools for use in the classroom. Yet, when she was head of the children's room at the New York Public Library (1906 to 1941), she was forced to recognize that school services had become a major part of her staff's work. She appointed a supervisor of service to schools in 1918 to coordinate activities and the loaning of books to teachers (Sayers 1972). Mabel Williams, a librarian from Massachusetts, helped Anne Carroll Moore develop the work the NYPL did with schools, declaring independence from school-type instruction within the library's walls. Class visits to the library evolved, with more emphasis on spirited book talks and the promotion of voluntary reading.

The School Library Movement Begins (1890 to 1940)

Although most librarians and teachers were women, administrative posts in institutions and in professional associations were predominantly held by men, such as Melvil Dewey and John Cotton Dana. While Dewey's contributions have become legendary and are remembered on a daily basis through our use of the Dewey Decimal System, evidence of Dana's influence has remained hidden in the historical records of the American Library Association (ALA) and the National Education Association (NEA). Dana, however, was greatly instrumental in providing solid library service to schools.

Dana, who was trained as a lawyer and not as a librarian, fell into librarianship in 1889 at the Denver Public Library. Dana had previously written and published articles on a wide variety of topics, and his opinions on education became well known throughout Denver. The superintendent of the Denver public schools and the school board recognized Dana's knowledge and potential and appointed him to be the librarian in charge of the public library being built as part of the East Denver High School building. This arrangement, with the public library being physically and administratively connected to the school, was not unheard of but was still unique. The library had three reading rooms and a museum and was located on the ground floor of the west wing of the East Denver High School (Pond 1982). Even though the library was funded through tax support from the Denver School District Number One, everyone referred to the library as the Denver Public Library. As a result of Dana's strong interest in education, the Denver Public Library began lending collections of books to teachers for use as "school libraries" in their classrooms. These school libraries were really classroom collections of books on topics being covered in class.

The arrangement in Denver was more the exception than the rule in the nineteenth and early-twentieth centuries. Overall, at this time few official school libraries or librarians existed in the United States. Those school collections that did exist were small because there was no steady source of income for library materials or staff; teachers and students did not have much access to supplementary books. Until school collections became established, public library service to schools was practical and necessary.

Sometimes a teacher would act as the librarian at her school. Lutie Stearns, a self-proclaimed radical, taught school to seventy-two "fourth-reader" children in Milwaukee, Wisconsin, in the 1880s. The school had no library, and Stearns's classroom had only one book. Stearns constructed bookcases out of soap boxes and filled them with donated books. She also earned money by giving stereopticon lectures on Germany and used the money to purchase periodicals for use in her classroom. In addition to setting up a permanent classroom library, Lutie Stearns went the extra mile for her students' reading development by traveling to the Milwaukee Public Library every Thursday:

> On Thursday evenings, accompanied by three boys with six market baskets, she took the "horse car" to the Milwaukee Public Library, where she borrowed two books for each child: one of "wholesome fiction" and one "along the lines through which the child might discover his life interest." (Pawley 2000)

After providing this service to her students for two years, Lutie Stearns changed her career focus from teaching to librarianship and campaigned for the establishment of public and traveling libraries throughout Wisconsin.

Surveys conducted in the 1890s show that two-thirds of public libraries in the United States and Canada allowed teachers to check out collections of books for their students to use in the classroom or at home and that one-third of public libraries sent librarians to the public schools to do classroom visits. Many of the larger public libraries employed one or more librarians to work exclusively with the public schools (Jenkins 1996).

Mary E. Hall, the librarian at the Brooklyn Girls High School, was one of the strongest advocates for school library development and cooperation between the National Education Association and the American Library Association. In 1915, she and other school librarians successfully lobbied to establish the School Library Section. This section enabled school librarians to become organized and make contacts, helping the specialized profession come into its own during the twenties and thirties. Hall defined the school librarian as a "unique and essential educator working with other educators" (Barron 1995). School librarians began emphasizing their roles as leaders and managers in their schools. To foster use of media, these teacher-librarians needed to work hand in hand with classroom teachers, developing curricular units together.

School librarians worked toward standardizing their professional goals across the country, yet no consistent pattern emerged. Library and school districts developed local plans to best meet the information needs of their communities. In Illinois, for example, the Haven School library functioned as a branch of the Evanston Public Library for the community after the school closed for the day. When the school librarian, Mildred L. Batchelder, finished work at the end of the school day, public librarians came in to take her place for the late afternoon and evening. This arrangement resulted from cooperative efforts of the public library and the board of education. The public library hoped the school superintendents would see how valuable school libraries were, leading to funds to cover materials and operating costs. Batchelder, whose notable career was only in its infancy during her time at Haven School, felt that after the public library demonstrated the value and need for a school library, it should "get out and let the schools take over their own libraries" (Anderson 1981). Many school librarians longed for independence and the opportunity to establish their own identity as a profession. School and public libraries, as distinct institutions, had different missions, leading the librarians working at these institutions to develop specialized work patterns, values, and objectives.

Influences from Outside Librarianship
(1920 to 1940)

Meanwhile, developments in educational philosophy and changing trends in the publishing of books for youth exerted their influence on both public and school librarians. Lucy Sprague Mitchell was a reformer interested in progressive education. Beginning in 1919 Mitchell committed herself to the development of the Bank Street School in New York City. The school was experimental in nature and emphasized observing early child development, especially in the acquisition of language, paying special note to rhythm, rhyme, and other musical elements. While working and playing with young children in the Bank Street's nursery school, Mitchell listened to the children, collected thousands of their linguistic fragments, and analyzed the relationship between language development and a child's emerging identity.

If one looks back at the history of literature, one finds that nursery or Mother Goose rhymes were often sung to babies and children. Ancient oral stories such as Homer's *Iliad* and *Odyssey* were sung by a bard, whose performances combined music and the rhyme and rhythm of language. Folk and fairy tales, which also originated from oral tradition, often include short rhymes and songs that are repeated (sometimes with variations) throughout the story. If one has ever told a folktale with one of these rhymes or songs, one has noticed that children remember and repeat those sections for weeks after they have heard the story.

Mitchell's attention to the musical and playful aspects of language led her to disagree with the theories of noted child psychologists such as Jean Piaget. In Mitchell's view, Piaget believed that children outgrew the love of rhythm, sound quality, and playfulness in their language as they learned to use words to be understood by others. When children used language for semantic meaning instead of for play, they had reached a more mature developmental level. Mitchell, in contrast, claimed that when children were permitted to express themselves freely, they continued playing with language and rhythms as they grew older:

> To Piaget, this dropping of art elements from language is progress, is overcoming of immaturity. To me it is tragedy, for to me a child's pleasure in rhythm, sound quality and pattern is the seed from which literature grows. (Mitchell quoted in Marcus 1992)

Mitchell's emphasis on the art elements in language may remind one of Anne Carroll Moore's aesthetic focus in her work as a librarian: in collection development, Moore demanded aesthetic excellence in the books chosen for the library's collection; in school visits, she drew parallels between the work of the librarian and that of the musician, asking that the librarians strive to imitate the violin player, who was at one with his art; and, finally, Moore encouraged her staff to learn the art of storytelling and hired expert storytellers to be part of the permanent staff at the New York Public Library.

Although both Moore and Mitchell recognized the importance of art and aesthetics in children's development, they held opposing views on the types of literature made available to the young. Mitchell, whose educational ideals broke away from the traditional notion that children needed only lessons in discipline, the three Rs, and civics, also advocated the creation of a new kind of literature for the young.

In 1921 Mitchell's *Here and Now Story Book* was published. It included stories written in the repetitive, playful language Mitchell heard children using themselves. Most notably, the stories took place in an urban environment. Leonard Marcus (1992) describes how Mitchell's stories challenged accepted notions of appropriate literature for children:

> Much of children's literature of the period remained rooted in nineteenth-century Romanticism, with its idealized imagery of the happy child at home in harmonious natural surroundings. In stark contrast, Mitchell's stories about skyscrapers and airplanes, tugboats and trolleys acknowledged the demographic and social reality that in 1921 the majority of American children lived in cities.

Before Mitchell's research and writing at Bank Street, librarians and publishers widely believed that the literature of long ago, including fairy tales and myths, was the best introduction to literature. When the *Here and Now Story Book* appeared, Anne Carroll Moore condemned it as poor literature. Mitchell admitted that she herself did not have excellent writing talent or ability and declared that the great writer of "Here and Now" stories was still to be found (Marcus 1992).

Margaret Wise Brown, who joined the Bank Street School as a student teacher in 1935, became the great writer Mitchell had needed to write the "Here and Now" stories. Brown began writing children's books during creative writing seminars led by Mitchell at Bank Street; some of her early titles include *When the Wind Blew, Bumble Bugs and Elephants: A Big and Little Book,* and *The Little Fireman.* Having observed children for two years at Bank Street, Brown had developed a close connection to children's interests and psychology, often on an unconscious level. Unlike Mitchell, Margaret Wise Brown paid close attention to her own unconscious, inner life. She noted and examined the content of her dreams and felt that these types of inner resources should never be ignored by a writer. Even though Brown's stories differ greatly from fairy tales and myths, they exhibit a strong concern for the child's inner self.

The "Here and Now" stories by Lucy Sprague Mitchell and Margaret Wise Brown, having been critiqued by Anne Carroll Moore, often did not receive positive reviews. Through her position as head of the children's room at the New York Public Library, Anne Carroll Moore had a tremendous impact on the types of books being published for youth:

> Under Moore's leadership the selection of books for the Central Children's Room was never a casual affair. A New York Public Library purchase order soon came to be regarded as a major critical endorsement. In 1911 Moore formalized the matter, and greatly enhanced her power, by issuing the first of the library's annual fall lists of new books recommended for holiday gift giving. Such was her reputation nationally that inclusion on the list all but assured a book a respectable sale; omission might just as easily mean oblivion. (Marcus 1992)

In addition to endorsing or denouncing titles, Moore also exerted her influence by passing on her criteria to those she trained. These followers later became responsible for the selection of children's books at New York City's branch libraries as well as at public libraries throughout the country.

The New York Public Library's Central Children's Room housed a spectacular display of rare editions of fairy tales. Traditional tales, myths, fantasies, and legends helped, Moore believed, children reach "higher truths." The "Here and Now" stories, by contrast, were grounded in scientific theories, which Moore thought destroyed aesthetic creation. Leonard Marcus (1992) describes Moore's and Mitchell's philosophical differences:

> The librarian was a moral idealist who regarded childhood as a fixed state of innocence to be shielded from, rather than shaped by, historical change and environmental factors. Moore remained deeply suspicious of Mitchell's empirically grounded—and thus relativistic—"modern" approach to literature and education. Mitchell, for her part, was convinced that people like Moore lived in a sentimental dreamworld.

On one side of this debate, Moore and her followers emphasized the inner child and the child's imaginative life, which could be enriched through exposure to traditional literature such as fairy tales, myths, and legends. Mitchell and other progressive educators argued in favor of stories representing children's lived experiences. While teachers used Mitchell's *Here and Now Story Book* in their classrooms, children's rooms at public libraries offered story times featuring the retelling of folk and fairy tales.

The debate was often referred to as the Fairy Tale War and was much discussed at conferences and written about in library journals during the 1930s. In examining the children's librarians' viewpoint, it is important to remember the fervor of those establishing the profession during the Progressive Era. These librarians worked with missionary zeal to help educate and enrich the lives of children living in poverty—those experiencing the worst in squalid city conditions. By providing quality literature and pleasant surroundings in the public library, children's librarians strove to offer hope and eventual escape from the harsh realities of city life. When the "Here and Now" stories first appeared, the idea of representing reality, which for many was a dangerous, noisy, disease-infested city, ran counter to the Progressive Era mission to inspire hope and optimism. On the other hand, the "Here and Now" books did not emphasize negative aspects but instead focused on a child's open and enthusiastic view of exciting, contemporary city life.

The issue of realism in youth literature was and continues to be complex. Frances Clarke Sayers, who began her career as a children's librarian at the New York Public Library under Anne Carroll Moore and later taught children's literature at the University of California at Berkeley's library school, gave a speech in 1937 entitled "Lose Not the Nightingale" on the power of imaginative literature for children. This speech was in response to the newer, realistic books coming out for children. Sayers's speech was so popular among children's librarians that it had to go into a third printing. Christine Jenkins (1996) describes some of the interpretations of this speech:

> Some saw the "real nightingale" of children's literature as the salvation of humanity in a soulless world of industry and war; to them the cry to "lose not the nightingale" spoke of their determination to hold onto spiritual values at a time of stress and dislocation. Others, however, questioned the wisdom of taking the time to listen to the real nightingale in a world that appeared to be rushing into another world war. Of what good was a real nightingale, however sweetly it sang, if it did not give children the information they needed about the all-too-real world of poverty, violence, and injustice that lay right outside their door?

Over time, teachers and both school and public librarians reached a consensus, acknowledging that a variety of literary genres—fairy tales, fantasy, realistic fiction, biographies, picture books on construction trucks and airplanes—play a role in meeting the psychological and educational needs of youth. Yet it is important to note that this point of tension in the 1920s and 1930s had far-reaching consequences for those in the fields of education and librarianship. One's position on the definition of quality literature for youth could, at this time, show allegiance to a particular profession. School librarians began to ally themselves more with teachers and with what teachers felt their students needed (that is, "here and now" books as well as titles helpful for teaching reading). Studies show, however, that both types of librarians bought basically the same books for their libraries (Jenkins 1995). Yet, the fact that school librarians *saw* themselves and their profession as different from public librarians and their profession was one of the key factors leading to tension between the two groups.

School and Public Librarians Go Their Separate Ways (1940 to 1960)

In her position as Chief of the School and Children's Library Division and later as the Executive Secretary of the Division of Libraries for Children and Young People (DLCYP), Mildred Batchelder worked ceaselessly as an advocate and source of information for both school and public children's librarians. During these years (1936 to 1966) working at ALA headquarters, Batchelder emphasized the related rather than the distinct aspects of these professions' missions. She saw great value in public children's librarians and school librarians spending time together, sharing ideas, and discovering ways to cooperate. Throughout her long career, she was consistent on one crucial point: all librarians, no matter what their specialty or place of work, could benefit from seeing their work as part of the larger whole of librarianship in general; just as school and public librarians should not alienate themselves from each other, public youth services librarians needed to be careful not to isolate themselves from the rest of the staff at their libraries.

Although Batchelder contributed much to the development of school librarianship as a profession, many school librarians did not share her unifying philosophy. During the war years, new leaders in school librarianship emerged and strongly asserted that school librarians and public children's librarians had distinct roles and responsibilities; this was a time for acknowledging differences rather than noting similarities. Mary Hall's early vision of the school librarian as a "unique and essential educator working with other educators" became the vision of many. School librarians emphasized their roles as leaders and managers as well as the importance of integrating curriculum and media in the schools (Barron 1995).

During the promotion of and the justification for school libraries in the 1930s and 1940s, tension between school and public librarians increased exponentially. Part of this tension resulted from economic factors. Having less money after the Depression, taxpayers were less willing to support both school and public libraries. As a result, each institution had to defend itself. During this defense, issues on professional jurisdiction and philosophical differences between school and public libraries came to the forefront. Frances Henne, a librarian at the University of Chicago Laboratory High School, said that many librarians believed that the children's department at the public library was a "vestigial remain" and that all library services for children should be transferred to the schools (Anderson 1981). Unfortunately, some public library administrators held the same belief and hoped that funding that was being used for youth materials could be transferred to develop better adult collections. Batchelder seriously questioned this turn of events and urged school and public librarians to clarify their roles, shift their objectives as libraries changed, and work together to expand and improve library services for children, whether those children were in or out of school.

Cooperation was also urged by Robert D. Leigh, a political scientist who headed a study in the late 1940s called the *Public Library Inquiry* to discover how public libraries contributed to society. The publications of his findings on the various levels of school-library cooperation led to heated discussion and debate. During numerous talks about his findings, Leigh asked school and public librarians to end their competition by striving toward common wages and common training. He also tried to reassure them by stating that youth needed cooperative library services provided by both school and public libraries. Even though Leigh encouraged public and school librarians to work together, his findings and talks underscored the differences between the two groups:

> He commended public children's librarians for their superior knowledge of children's literature, and commended school librarians' superior salaries, benefits, and vacations. Not surprisingly, Leigh's comments raised the hackles of both school and public librarians. . . . While the *Public Library Inquiry* certainly did not create the split between school and

public librarians, the report, with its lack of research on services to children and young people and its recommendations for increased school library service, served to heighten tensions between the two groups. (Jenkins 1995)

School librarians allied themselves with teachers and distanced themselves from public librarians by emphasizing their role in curriculum and instruction. Frances Henne supported a "problem-centered curriculum" that emphasized contemporary social issues. This curriculum required that teachers and students move away from total dependence on textbooks and use supplementary materials from the school library (Jenkins 1995). The school librarians' role in this type of curriculum necessitated their becoming more involved in educational associations and coming to understand the needs of teachers.

Unrest grew among school librarians because they sensed that others—including public children's librarians, administrators at ALA, and teachers—did not understand their issues and problems. This growing unrest soon led to rebellion, stimulated by the ALA reform to restructure and reduce the number of divisions in the association. Although the reform, for the most part, did not come to pass, the school librarians did establish a separate division in ALA, the American Association of School Librarians (AASL), in 1951. In the process, they also fired Mildred Batchelder as their executive secretary and hoped for a fresh start with new leadership. Even though Batchelder had devoted much of her professional life to advocating for and developing school librarianship, the school librarians felt that she sided with the public librarians during any conflict over status within ALA when, in fact, Batchelder only hoped to keep all librarians working with youth in contact with one another, in a unified organization. Batchelder, who had worked hard to establish harmony among these librarians, was deeply hurt when the AASL informed her that they did not want her to represent them.

Public librarians tended to view this separatist movement negatively, having long believed that youth librarians had gained strength through unity. In dividing into two separate groups, they would lose what they had gained through cooperation. They also saw Frances Henne, who believed library service to children should be handled by the schools, as an enemy to the profession (Anderson 1981). School librarians, by contrast, held affection and respect for Henne because she understood their struggles and represented their point of view.

During this time of strife, many association members concentrated so much on organizational status that they overlooked what school and public librarians had in common and failed to notice that Batchelder and Henne and the groups they represented actually held the same viewpoints on primary issues: placing the right book into the hand of the right child at the right time, advocating for intellectual freedom, promoting quality literature, and encouraging lifelong use of the library for continued learning.

The Blackboard Curtain and Beyond
(1960 to Today)

As the preceding brief history illustrates, the missions of public children's librarians and school librarians were closely interwoven yet still distinguishable. If we define the unique characteristics of each specialty, we notice different emphases in mission but no clear-cut boundaries.

The public librarian tended to focus on encouraging youth to read for pleasure. Public library children's rooms were welcoming places where children would come voluntarily to pursue their interests independently. By exploring high-quality books, children would come to know beauty and art and have joyful experiences at the library. The concept of freedom—whether freedom from a schedule, from a prescribed lesson, or from required reading lists—was at the heart of public library faith. Youth were encouraged to come and go spontaneously, to find their own rhythm of visiting the library, and to browse the shelves and choose their own books. By making their own choices, young patrons developed skills in discrimination and judgment. If help was needed, the librarian was readily available to suggest an appropriate book or help find material for a homework assignment. This librarian was not, however, the same type of authority figure as a teacher or parent but, instead, more closely resembled an older sister, brother, aunt, or uncle who was knowledgeable about books for youth.

The school setting required school librarians to align their mission with the overall mission of the school. Mary Hall's concept of a "unique and essential educator working with other educators" to integrate curriculum and media proved to be greatly influential from the time of Hall's presidency of the NEA Library Department in 1912 through the twentieth century. In a 1966 article entitled "Learning to Learn in School Libraries," Henne expands Hall's vision by explaining how this "unique and essential educator" could play a central role in the school:

> Serves on school's curriculum committee, plans with administrators and teachers
>
> Teaches students how to use library and its resources

Analyzes assignments and curricular content in order to determine the types of study and research skills that need to be taught

Teaches students how to use audiovisual equipment, how to view, listen, perceive, and evaluate

In general, a school librarian has been and continues to be joined—body, mind, and spirit—to the school curriculum, with most of her work being dictated in some way by that curriculum. The school librarian also encourages students to read for pleasure and keeps track of students' interests, recommending books to expand and develop those interests. In the previously mentioned article, Frances Henne emphasizes the school librarian's proximity to the students and the opportunity for him or her to observe students' abilities and interests carefully and offer personal guidance. She claims that much lack of staff in school libraries has "led to an over-emphasis on teaching and requiring students to work independently in libraries" (Henne 1966). We find this theory of close guidance resurfacing again today in the discussion of the school's in loco parentis role and Internet filtering issues.

Tensions between school and public librarians continued in the 1960s and 1970s partially due to the growth of population in the United States. Babies born in the post–World War II era had grown up to be elementary- and high-school students. These students began coming in droves to the public library after school to hang out and to work on their homework assignments. Since public libraries were not equipped to cope with this increased business, many new policies were instituted that negatively affected service to students. This lack of service came to be known as the "blackboard curtain." In the introduction to her book *Creating the Full-Service Homework Center in Your Library*, Cindy Mediavilla (2001) describes how students were treated in the 1960s and 1970s:

> According to findings revealed at the 1967 American Library Association (ALA) Conference, young people's borrowing privileges were being restricted nationwide. Reference service to students was curtailed or denied altogether; library use permits were required from teachers or parents or both; teenagers were limited to certain hours and areas of the library; and boys and girls in many towns were not allowed to use their local libraries on the same evening.

This "student problem" arose out of exhaustion on the part of public librarians attempting to meet an unprecedented demand for their services.

In addition, the tension between school and public librarians most likely contributed to confused roles and attitudes. Tired public librarians began to place responsibility on school libraries, assuming they could fill all the educational needs of students. Some librarians even thought that school and homework support at public libraries would be detrimental to the further development of school libraries.

During the 1980s rapid technology changes forced librarians to see the interrelationships of the services offered by all libraries, whether school, academic, or public. Today, in the age of the "library without walls," we all depend on one another, linking to one another's' Web sites and sharing electronic resources. In addition, the public library has, in general, accepted its role in literacy training and homework assistance. One hopeful sign of school–public library cooperation is the flourishing of homework centers in public libraries across the country.

As the public librarian incorporates the mission of providing resources at the public library for students to complete homework assignments, the school librarian promotes reading for pleasure through storytelling, free reading time, Poetry Month, and Battle of the Books. Yet, school librarians have many new responsibilities, especially those related to computers. They now may rely more heavily on public librarians to promote reading for pleasure in their communities. Public libraries also have their limitations. Even though the public librarian continues to stay up-to-date on the local schools' curricula and purchases materials accordingly, curriculum support is only one of a public library's many roles. The youth services department in a public library must also provide materials for preschoolers and parents, as well as materials on non-school-related topics to fill other informational needs—whether those needs are educational, recreational, or spiritual. To fill this wide variety of needs, public libraries generally (but not always, depending on funding) rely on the school libraries to provide primary service to teachers and students on school-related projects. The public library does, however, try to have as many materials as possible on hand to help with standard homework assignments and may have other supplementary materials available for independent research projects. So the missions of school and public librarians do not contradict each other but are, instead, complementary.

The next chapter outlines the typical strengths of school and public libraries and describes how we can make use of those strengths on a daily basis to serve youth better.

2 Different Strengths, Common Goals

As discussed in the previous chapter, library media specialists and public librarians share common goals and core professional values. Both professions dedicate themselves to encouraging young people to read for pleasure, to read quality literature, to develop independent research skills, and to use the library for continuous, lifelong learning. This section will outline some practical suggestions for using our different strengths to meet these common goals.

PROMOTING INFORMATION LITERACY

The teaching and promotion of information literacy has become an increasingly important goal of libraries. In an information-rich society, we are required to evaluate resources when making decisions about our work, our health care, our political views, as well as in many other areas of our lives. Information literacy skills enable us to have satisfying and productive lives and contribute, with thought and knowledge, to our democratic society. Librarians everywhere strive to prepare people to be independent, lifelong learners who recognize the need for accurate information. For people of all ages in the community, excellent library service is provided when school, public, and other (including corporate and hospital) librarians work together and refer individuals to whichever library or librarian can best answer a question. We hope to live as a community of learners, with access to many library collections and online databases. As we teach patrons basic information skills in various locations, the community can move beyond asking basic questions (where is the dictionary?) to more evaluative questions (which dictionary is the best to use for this situation?). In forming alliances with each other, libraries can improve the overall information literacy of our communities.

School and public librarians will greatly enhance the education of the community's young by learning how the services they offer can complement and support each other. In the past, the curriculum orientation of school libraries set them apart from public libraries. School librarians have been teaching information literacy skills since about 1938 and have worked with teachers since that time to create and implement instructional programs for students in elementary, middle, and high schools (Grassian and Kaplowitz 2001). Rapid changes in technology since the 1980s, however, forced public libraries to offer more thorough information literacy training. Now, more than ever before, both types of libraries have much in common in the teaching of information literacy skills and can greatly benefit from each other's expertise. In our fast, frantic, ever-changing world, information literacy is needed in every aspect of life and must be valued not only in schools and colleges but also by the entire community. The learning of these skills takes place at every age and at every library.

In the preschool years, children come to the public library for story time, where they are introduced to literature, art, and the sounds and rhythms of language. They also learn information literacy skills by observing others at the public library. They watch, for instance, their parents or caregivers talk with librarians and use online catalogs to find picture books featuring a favorite character or animal. Many children at this age even approach the librarian directly and ask questions about favorite books and topics. Public librarians can encourage comfort in a library setting by answering preschoolers' questions in an enthusiastic and friendly manner and by making eye contact with the preschooler. Preschoolers can also become skilled at using the computer mouse through playing recreational or educational games on the public library computers.

During their school years, students continue to use the public library but may use their school library more frequently due to its location. In good school libraries, the collection and instruction will help students learn information literacy skills while they are involved in a particular project related to the curriculum. For geography assignments, for example, students will learn how to use atlases as well as map resources available on the Internet. The library media specialist will prepare a formal lesson and guidelines for the students working on the project. In a public library, by contrast, the librarian will respond spontaneously to a student's particular questions and focus only on that question, informally modeling how to use an atlas or how to find a map on the Internet. Depending on the funding situation at their schools and in their community, students will find which library best helps them obtain the information and skills they need. Students cannot do this alone, however, and they need the guidance and cooperation of both school and public librarians.

Once students reach college age, they tend to use their college or university library for completing assignments and also, as they did in elementary school and high school, for recreational reading. Many college students continue to use the public library, especially for materials such as popular novels and videos. The public library becomes a patron's main library again when he or she leaves college and enters the workforce.

The advantage of the public library is its constant presence throughout life, while the advantage of the school library is its proximity and specialization. Librarians hope that students do not forget about libraries when they cease to be students; if school and academic libraries emphasize life-long learning in addition to the completion of assignments and promote use of the public library, this abandonment will be less likely to happen. Public librarians, in turn, must remember that school and academic libraries tend to have the best resources for school assignments and remind students to check their school's library for materials.

AN OVERVIEW OF THE STRENGTHS
OF SCHOOL AND PUBLIC LIBRARIES

The different yet complementary strengths of school and public libraries benefit every community. (Those strengths are summarized in table 2.1.) In terms of practical functionality, young people need school libraries as their principal resources for curricular material and as places to learn about resources and research methods. These libraries are located at a primary place of learning, where the collaboration of the school media specialist and the students' teachers can greatly enhance the effectiveness of school education by integrating the teaching of subject material with the practice of research techniques appropriate for a given subject and assignment.

TABLE 2.1
The Strengths of School and Public Libraries

School Libraries	Public Libraries
Close proximity to students, ease of access	Hours and days extend beyond times that school library is open
Frequent librarian-teacher interaction	Frequent librarian-parent interaction
Structured, thorough information literacy training	One-on-one, point-of-need information literacy training
Frequent, consistent contact between student and librarian	Library and staff have continuous presence throughout an individual's lifetime
Close guidance	Informal guidance
Literacy skills tied to daily schoolwork	Self-directed learning and discovery
Students can easily work together to share information-search strategies	Students witness modeling of library use by people of all ages
Library collection and instruction strongly connected to school district's educational goals	Library collection and programs strongly connected to community's needs

Being trained teachers, library media specialists can apply their excellent knowledge of child development and learning strategies to their daily work in the library, whether they are choosing the right books for the collection, telling a story, teaching a class about search engines, or keeping a feisty group of fifth graders focused. Through their frequent, consistent contact with all students, school librarians also have a more intimate understanding of the interests and motivations of a broad range of young readers and computer users. This daily connection can especially enable school librarians to take students' emotional needs into consideration when working with them. In most cases, the school librarian will be more aware of an individual's feelings and concerns than will a public librarian, yet there are always cases in which some students open up more with the public librarian. School librarians also communicate daily (though not to the extent they would hope) with classroom teachers and have an in-depth knowledge of curriculum.

Sharing this knowledge of curriculum is one of the best ways school librarians can help their local public libraries. Public librarians must infer, through reference questions, which topics are being studied. Since student use of the public library's resources after school and on weekends is often essential to the completion of assignments, the public library must own resources covering current curricular topics.

As soon as public librarians know which topics are to be covered, they can, in turn, assist the school librarian by offering further suggestions for resources to be purchased for the school library or to be placed on hold at the public library for the duration of an assignment. Public libraries generally have larger collections than school libraries, and public librarians, as a consequence, often are aware of a wide range of materials that may not be available in the schools. These librarians are experts at working with people of all ages in one-on-one situations and are familiar with the types of learning occurring in the community, outside the classroom. Their communication with school library media specialists can lead to more dialogue and emphasis on individualized learning and on connecting students' personal interests with academic projects.

LEARNING TO READ: BALANCING FREE READING WITH STRUCTURED LESSONS

The public librarian encounters many students who have come to the library voluntarily and who have a natural inclination for reading. To improve their reading skills, these children need little more than access to high-quality reading materials, a parent or other literate person to share the love of reading, and an occasional explanation of the meaning of an unfamiliar word.

My mother used to read to me every night, going as far back as I can remember. She taught me to read, inadvertently, when I was about four, beginning with *The Pineapple Duck with the Peppermint Bill,* by Lois Utz (1968). The book was in rhyme, and I soon had the story memorized. I still remember lines from it: "Once far away on the top of a hill / Lived a pineapple duck with a peppermint bill." As I told the story from memory, looking at the pictures, my mother pointed out on the page the shape of the words I was saying. I think I learned to read by osmosis because one day I could not read, and, suddenly, it seemed that I could. Today my four-year-old son memorizes rhymed picture books and asks me where certain words are printed on the page.

Since I learned to read with rhymed picture books, I have recommended them to parents hoping to teach their children to read, even though I know different children learn in different ways. Many of my colleagues at the public library follow a similar approach, recommending that parents, above all else, share quality books with their children. At the public library, we shy away from being too instructive about the process of learning to read. Instead, we ask children and parents which topics and authors they enjoy, ask the children what books they've read in the past, try to assess which books are too easy or too difficult, and recommend future books based on those answers.

Some teachers subscribe to a similar approach and emphasize free reading time in class and storytelling. This approach has been validated by research, succinctly described in *The Power of Reading: Insights from the Research,* by Stephen Krashen (1993). Krashen argues that free voluntary reading (FVR)—the kind of reading one does because one wants to—develops reading comprehension, spelling, vocabulary, grammar, and writing style more effectively than does traditional direct instruction. Many schools now incorporate FVR into each week or even into each day.

Due to their training in education, school librarians and teachers (especially reading teachers) are more aware of the issues surrounding the teaching of reading than is the typical public librarian. Like most public librarians (but not all), I was not an education major and had only a couple of education courses. Instead, as a literature major, my work focused on analyzing literary texts, becoming familiar with theories about aesthetics, and developing critical thinking and research skills.

Until I attended a Public Library Association (PLA) workshop in spring 2001, I had very little understanding of the importance of phonological awareness. The workshop began with a presentation of recent educational research by Reid Lyon from the National Institute of Child Health and Human Development. Lyon argued that reading is not a natural process; it is a skill that must be taught. More often than not, parents do a majority of such teaching. Children must acquire phonological awareness before they are able to read. Since the English language is seamless when spoken, all the teeny sounds fold into themselves. It is difficult for children to hear the different sounds and to realize that a letter or a combination of letters represents sound. Parents, according to Lyon, need to help their children segment and splice words, sometimes by syllable and other times by sounds of letters. Phonological awareness is best developed early through rhyming games and nursery rhymes. After children are able to link letters and sounds, they become speedy and fluent readers and have no trouble decoding text. At that point, authentic literature and the whole language approach should be used.

I realized that my intuitive approach of recommending picture books with rhyming or cumulative text was not entirely off base. Yet, at the same time, I learned that all those "boring" books about a single letter in the alphabet were much more valuable than I had believed. Ever since I attended the PLA workshop, my recommendations for very beginning readers have changed. In addition to giving a few suggestions about excellent picture books and other books to read aloud, I direct parents and children (in preschool and kindergarten) to those books focusing on the sounds of letters or combinations of letters. I have also requested many alphabet games and other displays of the alphabet for use in the play area of our department.

This experience helped me recognize that my education had some holes and that I, like many public librarians, need to make a concentrated effort to stay up-to-date and consider how to integrate the results of new research into daily work. School librarians can help us by recommending appropriate articles and workshops. Public librarians, in turn, can help those school librarians who have had only a few courses in literature or library science stay up-to-date on literary trends, research techniques, and the evaluation of resources.

In a perfect world, both public and school librarians would cover the same material in library school and would become equally versed in educational psychology, literary analysis, teaching methods, and resource evaluation. Yet many public librarians have had insufficient course work in education because they did not plan to become teachers and either did not foresee the value of such courses or did not have time to take them due to the requirements for their chosen majors. School librarians, on the other hand, are often former classroom teachers who have an excellent background in education but have taken very few library science courses (if they have not completed a master's degree in library science) to become certified to work as the school librarian. We all have gaps in our professional preparation and, instead of criticizing each other, we need to reach out to each other to fill in the holes and make good recommendations for continuing education.

So, given that students benefit from the knowledge of both public and school librarians, how do we work together to make the most of our strengths? As in all cooperative efforts, we begin by getting to know each other and communicating on a regular basis. The next chapter provides practical tips for initiating contacts to encourage collegiality and, eventually, collaborative projects.

3 Everyday Practice

A How-to Guide

INITIATING CONTACT

To initiate contact, one may instinctively decide to stop by another library and introduce oneself informally. Often, dropping off information such as bibliographies or brochures advertising a reading program can be a good first step in the introduction process. If a public librarian suddenly shows up at a school library, however, and hopes *to get to know* the librarian, she or he will most likely be sadly disappointed and experience a rushed encounter. School librarians usually teach during the day, and public librarians may not know a convenient time to visit. Similarly, if a school librarian stops by the public library after school to meet the staff, introductions and conversations may be interrupted several times because public libraries are especially busy at that time. The best plan is to set up a time when all parties can get away from their daily work and focus on each other entirely, without interruption.

ARRANGING A GET-ACQUAINTED PARTY

1. Find a time likely to be convenient for both school librarians and public librarians. Often the time between the end of summer reading and

the beginning of the school year allows more flexibility than other times of the year.

2. Obtain administrative support for your event. If the library director or principal supports the effort, he or she can contact administrators at the other institution and encourage their support as well.

3. Reserve a room for the event.

4. Make your guest list. Generally, if the goal is getting acquainted, the more people you invite, the better. For specific projects, you will probably want to invite only those who are directly involved. But, at the beginning, you have no idea who might be involved, so invite as many people from the staffs at each library as you can. If you are a school librarian, invite the librarians at the public library as well as librarians and their assistants from other schools in your district and perhaps even from neighboring school districts. If you are a public librarian, invite the school librarians and assistants from all schools in the area served by your library as well as the staff of your library. While making your list, call and find out the names (with correct spellings) of the guests.

5. Decide who will help with the event. Get together and discuss food and beverages and decorations. Plan as elegant an event as your budget allows. We often use the china donated to us by the former local Women's Club when that group disbanded. The floral plates and cups help our guests feel special and welcome and add a touch of fun.

6. Assemble packets of information about your library or school. Include an introductory brochure about your institution as well a list of staff members and their e-mail addresses or telephone extensions. If you work in a school, include information about your school's mission and curriculum and special projects for the coming year. If you work in a public library, include some brochures on reading programs as well as bibliographies appropriate for elementary-, middle-, and high-school students. Information on special services available to teachers would be especially helpful.

7. Ask coworkers to make cookies and cakes for an afternoon tea, or, if your budget allows, plan a catered breakfast or lunch.

8. Send a personal invitation to each person. General invitations (such as "To Everyone at the Abigail Adams School Library") are not as effective as invitations to individuals. Include place, time, type of get-together, directions, and a contact person and phone number. A sample invitation is shown in figure 3.1.

FIGURE 3.1
Invitation

The Children's Department at the Ela Area Public Library
cordially invites you to the

Annual Spring Teacher-Librarian Tea
Thursday, May 23
3:00 to 5:00 p.m.

Please join us in the Children's Program Room, or if the weather permits, out on the patio. We will offer a tour of the new library at 3:30 p.m. highlighting areas of special interest to teachers. After the tour we will offer refreshments, information on our summer reading program, an overview of upcoming exhibits and programs appropriate for school groups, and best of all, friendly conversation.

We welcome any updates on your classroom curricula and look forward to hearing your suggestions for new library materials and programs.

Please RSVP to Natalie Ziarnik by Monday, May 20 so that we can plan accordingly.   phone (847) 438-3840 or e-mail nziarnik@eapl.org

9. If you are optimistic, base your estimated number of guests on RSVPs. Through experience, however, we have found that people tend not to RSVP much for these events. You might want to make some friendly reminder calls and ask about the number of people who are planning to come.

10. Prepare or order food, purchase or make decorations, and prepare a display or two for the room so that people have something to look at and talk about.

11. On the day of the event, set out name tags and pens at the entrance to the room where the event is taking place and station a greeter at your building's front door to direct the guests to the proper room.

12. During the event, offer some informal tours of your facility. Exchange business cards, but otherwise do not focus on business. The purpose of this type of get-together is to promote friendship, familiarity, and easy communication in the future.

At the party, you have the opportunity to meet and talk with many people you encounter (almost anonymously) in daily work. Your hospitality at the party sets a precedent for your future relationships. Since you now know these colleagues better, you will meet, phone, and e-mail them with more enthusiasm and cheer. In addition, if at first you have no ideas on how working together can benefit local students, you will find that social get-togethers and increased contact will illuminate others' needs as well as their capabilities and inspire joint projects. For best results, make a follow-up plan to your initial meeting. What will the next step be? It could be anything from another casual meeting to an invitation to a staff meeting to the beginning of a librarians' book discussion group.

Your creativity will lead you to many other ways to get together. Perhaps you live in the same neighborhood as another librarian. When you see each other, take time to stop and chat about the weather, your gardens, or your children. Maybe you'll meet a future collaborator at a conference while talking about favorite authors. Follow up your meeting by calling the other person and recommending more favorite books. Most important, remember that we all need to keep ourselves open to new friendships and ways to share ideas and efforts to promote the best possible library service to young people.

If you plan an event and only a few guests arrive, do not dwell on those who are absent. You can look for other opportunities to work with them later. Instead of being disappointed, focus on building positive relationships with those who have responded to your invitations. Friendship and good-will will spread before long. Overall, it is less stressful to start small, begin with simple cooperative efforts, and then build on those efforts. If you have the motivation and time to do more, you can subsequently consider asking for administrative support to do more involved collaborative projects. Just remember: every small effort has a ripple effect. When you start small, you are more likely to continue the project to completion. In *A Single Shard,* by Linda Sue Park (2001), Crane-man gives some advice to Tree-ear, a young orphan about to embark on a long journey:

> Your mind knows that you are going to Songdo. But you must not tell your body. It must think one hill, one valley, one day at a time. In that way, your spirit will not grow weary before you have even begun to walk.

WORKING TOGETHER FOR THE FIRST TIME

Often one doesn't have the luxury of knowing people informally before working with them on a collaborative project. A public librarian may call the local school librarians and ask if they would be interested in helping her establish a Battle of the Books program next fall. A school librarian may contact a public librarian about teachers' requests to bring their classes to the public library for tours. Even in these down-to-business situations, the participants can work out the details more smoothly if they discuss plans over a cup of coffee and a slice of fresh banana bread.

Tips for Working Together

1. Become familiar with each colleague's schedule as well as the events and stresses in his or her typical day.
2. Respect each person's time and try to divide work as equally as possible. Sometimes a project will be sponsored primarily by one institution or another. Be clear if this is the case.
3. Consider which parts of the collaborative work will make use of your strengths and expertise.
4. Respect each colleague's strengths and expertise as well. You will soon discover how your talents and knowledge complement each other.

5. Be practical. A public librarian cannot expect a school librarian to come frequently on tours just as the school librarian cannot expect the public librarian to teach library skills to classes for an entire week. Collaborative work should fit within the structure of each participant's normal work and the mission of his or her home institution. Cross-over is necessary, but it should not become excessive.

CONTINUING CONTACT

As you get to know your colleagues at other libraries, you'll be surprised how often your work will bring you together. Keep contact information for your new colleagues close at hand and zip off an e-mail message whenever you encounter an excellent resource or need advice on collection development decisions. One easy way to stay in contact is to send each other monthly newsletters. School librarians and teachers can help the public library stay current on school events while public librarians can send information about holiday craft programs or announce additions to the collection that would be of special interest to educators.

At public libraries, the usual contact people tend to be the children's, young adult, or reference librarians. Some larger libraries have one or two designated people who communicate and work with the local schools. At the Queens Borough Public Library, the Coordinator of Community Youth Services administers the Connecting Libraries and Schools Project (CLASP). This coordinator works closely with the Offices of School Library Services and the Central Board of Education in New York City (Fitzgibbons 2001). In most Chicago suburban public libraries, a librarian designated as a school liaison or school facilitator focuses primarily on service to teachers and students. When budgeting allows for such positions, work with the schools becomes more organized and is given a higher priority. Even in those libraries with small staffs, it is best to give schools only one or two contact names at the public library to prevent confusion.

In smaller public libraries, staff members' positions are less specialized, and the children's librarian often responds to school needs in addition to performing his or her many other duties. Even very small public libraries can provide excellent service to schools. Amy Gee works at the Carthage Public Library, a relatively new library with only part-time staff, in Carthage, Illinois. Amy offers orientation to the library to first and third graders every spring and gives book talks to all fourth-, fifth-, sixth-, seventh-, and eighth-grade classes. Since the elementary schools do not have libraries or librarians in Carthage, the public library service is essential. The town's high school does have a librarian; however, she is primarily committed to managing the school district's computers and does not have time to visit classrooms and promote reading. In this type of situation, public librarians and teachers need to work closely together to encourage students to read for pleasure, to ensure adequate curriculum support, and to lobby for the funding of libraries and librarians in the elementary schools.

After establishing your contacts, begin a tradition, such as a monthly or annual breakfast, at which all related staff from the schools and public libraries get together to eat, socialize, and exchange information. (See the librarian-teacher tea described in the chapter 9 for more specific ideas.) Such get-togethers keep everyone informed of community events, new books and services, and changes in personnel. Most important, regular interaction encourages communication and collegiality, which directly leads to better service to our students.

4 Grants

Grants have provided many institutions with the inspiration to work collaboratively. Often the steps involved in applying for a grant require that one obtain support from others outside one's home institution. When a public library applies for a grant to receive money for a summer reading program, for example, the library may need to solicit letters of support for the program from faculty members at local schools. The process of asking for such letters builds rapport. All parties involved can then wait eagerly for the results, with the feeling that, no matter which local institution is awarded a grant, the entire community will benefit.

Before exploring sources of funding, you must clearly define your goals and the programs you plan to develop, the agencies you wish to include in your partnership, and the results you expect to achieve with your programs.

SOURCES OF GRANTS

Grants may be obtained from public or private sources. Sources of public funds include federal, state, and local agencies. Private funds come from charitable foundations, corporate support, and community organizations.

The Institute of Museum and Library Services

The Institute of Museum and Library Services (IMLS) offers nationally competitive federal grants for libraries and museums. It administers four grant programs for libraries: grants to state library agencies, grants to Native American library services, grants to Native Hawaiian library services, and national leadership grants for libraries. The IMLS also administers competitive grants called Library Services and Technology Act (LSTA) grants. Funding for LSTA grants is provided through state library agencies.

State Library Agencies

State library agencies offer grants specifically geared for libraries and are the best ones to begin with. Most state library agencies have a Web page listing grants and the deadlines for submitting application materials. These grants may be the most appropriate for libraries and are the easiest to apply for and receive. School libraries should apply for these library-oriented grants and also for grants sponsored by the U.S. Department of Education and state boards of education. Information about grants may only be sent to one's principal or library director, so school and youth services librarians should be sure to make their administrators aware of the interest in applying for grants.

Local Businesses

Local businesses can also provide monetary and other material support to libraries. Many youth services librarians are familiar with asking fast-food restaurants for coupons for free food or with approaching movie theaters or skating rinks for free passes for patrons who complete summer reading programs. Although it can be a little nerve-wracking and humbling to ask for donations from area businesses, most librarians are pleasantly surprised at the results. Businesses are usually more than willing to help their local community; art schools can offer free lessons to the winner of a library-sponsored art contest; bakeries can donate treats for open houses. If the library or school identifies the sponsoring businesses in newsletters and on posters promoting the event, the sponsors not only feel appreciated but also gain the goodwill of the community, which directly leads to more sales. Some larger businesses may have organized charitable programs and may be interested in sponsoring a homework center, complete with computers and other supplies. To find the appropriate contact person at a particularly large business, the resources listed at the end of the chapter should prove useful.

COLLABORATION IN GRANT EFFORTS

Ela Area Public Library

Many sources of grants encourage institutions to work with other institutions when implementing the programs to be funded by their grants. When the Ela Area Public Library was awarded Ela Books, Resources, Individuals Determining Goals for Educational Success (BRIDGES), an LSTA grant, for instance, the public library worked with the school district to arrange library tours for all fourth- and sixth-grade classes. The Ela Library applied for and received the grant, planned the tours, and, with the grant money, paid for the transportation necessary to bring the classes to the library. The teachers worked out the logistics of the transportation schedule, accompanied their students to the library, encouraged them to complete the library's scavenger hunt, and reinforced the literacy skills taught during the tours. As a result of the grant, hundreds of fourth- and sixth-grade students learned more about their local public library and brought their families back in the evenings and weekends to work on the scavenger hunt. Teachers became more aware of the library's resources, and the public library staff learned more about the information literacy needs of students and their families while assisting them with the scavenger hunt.

The Tall Tree Initiative in Westchester County, New York

One of the most notable school–public library programs takes place in Westchester County, New York, where the Reader's Digest Foundation provided a sizable grant to encourage schools and public libraries to join as "true partners in the educational process" through collaborative projects (Tarin and Turnbull 2001). The Tall Tree library consultant, Patricia Tarin, asks those participating in the collaboration to think of themselves as a "single support system for the student, not as two separate entities" (Rockfield 1998). All participants meet frequently and take the time to get to know each other personally and to understand each other's institutions. One acknowledged tendency is that "schools tend to be more formal and focused" because they face state mandates, whereas "libraries need the flexibility to deal with many different age groups and interests" (Rockfield 1998).

The Tall Tree Initiative has been very successful, leading to increased library use by students and a multitude of school–public library collaborative projects. The results of the venture have been published in a three-volume set entitled *Tall Tree: Sharing the Vision: How Schools and Libraries Can Work Together to Serve Children Better,* written by Patricia A. Tarin and Barbara Turnbull and published by the Reader's Digest Foundation.

Intergovernmental Cooperation in Bensenville, Illinois

If institutions have a history of working together well on past projects, applying for and obtaining grants can be much easier. The town of Bensensville, Illinois, has a long-standing practice of intergovernmental cooperation. The public library's first home was located in a reserved section of the Fenton High School library in 1957. When more space was needed, the library moved to other locations and, eventually, to its own new building. As the community grew through the years, the schools and the public library worked together, coordinating resources and building partnerships. In 1988, the elected officials and administrators of the five local taxing districts—Bensenville Community Public Library District, Bensenville Park District, Bensenville Elementary School District, Fenton High School District, and the village of Bensenville—formed the Bensenville Intergovernmental Group. This group met and continues to meet regularly to discuss visions and goals for Bensenville's future. The members of the group formed a strong bond in recognizing that they had common needs and purposes; just as importantly, they saw that they could count on each member's help and cooperation. In addition to forging professional relationships, the members had become friends.

As a result of these meetings, the group resolved to establish Bensenville as a community dedicated to lifelong learning. This philosophy was soon put to work when the school superintendent, Cesare Caldarelli Jr., and the library director, Jill Rodriguez, began discussing a joint construction project: a new building connected to the current public library that would house the educational administration center and a lifelong learning center. Through a Secretary of State Live and Learn Construction Grant, Bensenville was able to realize its dream, demonstrating how intergovernmental cooperation can enable a community to use resources effectively and efficiently. For this building, the school district and library district have worked out a way to share not only the space and staffing of the facility but also the costs for repairs, heating, and electricity.

Jill Rodriguez and Cesare Caldarelli envisioned this joint facility as a place where the following learning activities could take place:

Teachers develop new strategies and stay technologically up-to-date.

Parents model learning and improve their own life skills.

Students work independently, pursuing individual goals.

Library staff stimulates the development of research and learning skills through current technological tools. (Press publications, April 14, 1999)

From the early planning stages, the library director and the superintendent had a common dream and worked with leaders in technology, business, telecommunications, and education to design the center. Caldarelli's remarks typify the community's hopeful attitude about the future:

> Oftentimes, one sees a facility as an end in itself. I have never felt that way. I see this as a tool to build capacity for people. I will forever be proud when I think of people using this facility. I think all the time about teachers being in here and what they'll be able to do and how it will help them do their jobs better and to be more effective in working with children.

The joint facility is well used today and has expanded the types of cooperative projects conducted by the library and the school district. One unexpected advantage of the building's location was increased teacher-librarian communication. When students were in the lifelong learning center working on projects, their teachers began visiting the easily accessible (in the next room) public library. The teachers started talking frequently with the librarians, asking for assistance with research and informing the library staff of upcoming assignments. Through increased interaction, the library became more aware of what types of information literacy training teachers needed and began offering small-group training as well as all-day institutes.

Penny Mandziara, the school liaison librarian at Bensenville Community Public Library, and Jill Rodriguez, the library director, both emphasize that a willingness to give, to work together, is essential to cooperative work. If one goes the extra mile for others, the base of people one can count on becomes larger and larger. The library encourages this giving spirit by allowing their staff members to spend one hour of work time per week volunteering for Helping One Student to Succeed (HOSTS), a program that helps students to succeed by striving to raise their reading scores through one-on-one mentoring sessions. Nine library staff members participate in the program. The library board's willingness to allow the staff to do this on work time demonstrates the clarity of one of the community's missions: to promote lifelong learning through a personalized and cooperative approach. To learn more about daily work in Bensenville, see "A Day in the Life of Penny Mandziara " in chapter 8.

RESOURCES FOR GRANT SEEKERS

If you are a first-time grant seeker, the process may seem daunting. Some resources to help you get started are listed below. In addition, you may consider attending a grant-writing workshop to learn the basics. It is also helpful to partner with other people or agencies that are experienced in writing and administering grants. Depending on the scope of your project, you may also wish to hire a professional consultant to assist you with developing your proposal.

Guides to Grants for Libraries and Education

Taft Group for the American Library Association. 2002. *The Big Book of Library Grant Money 2002–2003*. Chicago: American Library Association.

Copublished biannually by the American Library Association and the Taft Group, this resource gathers all the library-specific funding programs from the broader, more expensive funding directories.

Foundation Center Staff, Gina-Marie Cantarella, eds. 2001. *National Guide to Funding for Libraries and Information Services*. 6th ed. New York: Foundation Center.

Gina-Marie Cantarella, ed. Foundation Center. 1999. *National Guide to Funding for Elementary and Secondary Education*. 5th ed. New York: Foundation Center.

The preceding are two of a number of specialized directories of foundations and corporate giving published biannually by the Foundation Center.

Guides to Grant Writing

Bauer, David G. 1999. *The "How-to" Grants Manual*. Rev. ed. Westport, Conn.: Greenwood.

New, Cheryl Carter, and James Aaron Quick. 1998. *Grantseeker's Toolkit*. New York: Wiley.

Internet Resources

In addition to the following sites, your state or regional library agencies may have Web sites with useful and valuable information about their programs. The Foundation Center offers a grant seeker's guide to resources, a basic primer on the grant-seeking process, and an introduction to the resources available. Available at: www.fdncenter.org/learn/ufg.

The U.S. Department of Education has a Web site listing information about which projects are being funded and who is receiving money. The site has useful contact names and addresses as well as excellent links to related agencies and interest groups. Available at: www.ed.gov.

5 Sharing Resources

GENERAL PROTOCOL FOR TEACHERS AND LIBRARIANS

As seen in the previous chapter on grants, schools and libraries can share spaces, staff, building expenses, computers, meeting rooms, and programming ideas. The most frequent form of resource sharing, however, remains the sharing of print and audiovisual materials. With the combined resources of the school and public libraries, teachers have many materials at their disposal. Our challenge is to find the best way to get the right resources to individual teachers as simply and quickly as possible. Since the school library is geographically closer than the public library, it is usually to the teacher's advantage to look for materials there first. By making the school library their first stop, teachers also help their school librarians know what types of materials are needed to support the classes in the school. This knowledge is crucial to ensure the development of an excellent collection appropriate for the individual school's curriculum and for the academic interests of its teachers.

When the school library does not have what the teacher needs, it is then time to contact the public library. Many teachers contact their public libraries themselves, but some school librarians prefer to request materials *for* the teachers. That way, the school librarian can check that the teacher has not overlooked materials placed on hold, hidden in the corner, or relegated to the repair shelf. If the material really is not available at the school, the librarian can then call the public librarian and ask to have it set aside or sent to the school for the teacher. If the same material is requested over and over, the school librarian will probably decide to purchase it for the school's collection. If the school librarian notices, however, that certain material is rarely needed, it is best for the library budget not to purchase such material and to put the money to better use. The book or video is easily accessible from the public library when it is needed. When teachers do not communicate with their school librarians and, instead, contact their public libraries first, the school librarians will not know which materials are most needed and the school collection will become less and less useful to teachers and their students.

School and public libraries can also share subscriptions to electronic databases. In some areas, a school is considered to be a patron of the public library and has its own library card number. Anyone attending or working in that school may use the card number to gain access to databases subscribed to by the public library. Often they will also need to contact the library to obtain the appropriate user name and password.

LIBRARIAN-TEACHER COMMUNICATION

School and public librarians share the many challenges of providing teachers and students with the right resources at the right time. Timing is of the utmost importance, and librarian-teacher communication is the only practical solution. Since teachers and school librarians work in the same building, it is possible for them to have frequent contact. Even so, teachers often do not tell their school librarians about current assignments or even changes in the topics they plan to cover in class during the semester. Instead, the school librarian may overhear teachers discussing their plans over lunch or in the hallways. Less frequently, though in a similar manner, the public librarian discovers information about assignments and curriculum topics indirectly. By the time the librarian hears about a curriculum change or an assignment, it is often too late to order new books or even to set aside currently owned books on the topic. In a matter of hours, just a few students may check out a library's entire collection of Civil War books, for example, and the remaining ninety students with the assignment are left with scant resources from reference books or nothing at all. This familiar situation has plagued all librarians at one time or another.

For years, librarians have attempted to use various assignment alert procedures to solve the problem. Teachers are asked to fill out a form about upcoming assignments, including a list of recommended resources for the students to use. After receiving these forms from the teachers, the school and public librarians may set aside some materials on temporary reserve so that students may have access to the material during their stay in the library. In other situations, the librarians may place a limit on how many books on a specified topic may be checked out by an individual, or they may shorten the lending period. In theory, such a system should work well. In reality, teachers are simply too busy to remember to send the required information to librarians on a consistent basis. Many librarians claim that giving an incentive (a free mouse pad, plant, or set of watercolors) to teachers who return assignment alert forms has proven effective. But, more often than not, teachers do not fill out the forms, and both school and public librarians must use other methods of discovering current and upcoming assignments.

An electronic service for posting homework assignments is available at www.yourhomework.com. Teachers type assignments on their own publicly accessible Web site so that students and parents may look up the information at home. Teachers can also send the information to the school library and local public libraries simply by clicking on appropriate boxes on the Web site. Since teachers are beginning to use e-mail and technology much more habitually than they did in the past, this electronic format could become successful.

HOMEWORK TIPS FOR TEACHERS

Some libraries, such as those in Durham, North Carolina, and Baltimore, Maryland, have prepared homework tips for teachers so that their students' trips to the library will be more rewarding and less frustrating. Many of the tips below are expanded versions of those listed in Cindy Mediavilla's book *Creating the Full-Service Homework Center in Your Library* (2001).

> Teachers can avoid a shortage of books by assigning a choice of reading options rather than requiring every student to read the same book.
>
> Teachers should avoid mass assignments on the same subject, especially if other classes have the same assignment.

Most importantly, teachers should visit the library and become aware of what materials are available there. Assignments can then be designed to be completed with the materials the library actually owns. It is not unusual for teachers to assume that particular materials are in publication when in fact they have yet to be written or are out of print.

Librarians can let teachers know about the various specialized encyclopedias available at the library. Both teachers and students may be aware of only general encyclopedias, such as *The World Book*, and may not realize that specialized encyclopedias can provide more information and may at times be the only source containing the material a student needs.

When teachers give students assignments in writing rather than orally, there is less chance that students, their parents, and librarians will misinterpret the purpose and requirements of an assignment.

Whenever possible, students should be given the opportunity to do research in the school library.

Librarians need to remind teachers that desired information may not be available for all reading levels. A library may have a book on tree frogs written at the third- or fourth-grade level, but it is entirely possible that no books on tree frogs have ever been written at the first-grade level.

Biography assignments can be particularly frustrating for librarians and students. It is not unusual for a teacher to require that students read a biography of at least one hundred pages. However, most biographies for elementary-school students consist of only forty to fifty pages, and then there is a huge leap to the regular, adult biographies, which can contain between three hundred and eight hundred pages. In addition, not as many biographies are written for elementary-school students as are written for older readers. Students cannot always choose to read a biography of any person who interests them. Before making a decision, they need to stop by the library and check the online catalog or call the library to see if an appropriate biography of their preferred person is available.

Writing and distributing brochures with guidelines for teachers can lead to increased understanding of what the library can and cannot offer. Yet, no technique is better than meeting with teachers face-to-face on a regular basis to discuss assignments and ways the library can contribute to student learning.

ALTERNATIVES TO ASSIGNMENT ALERT

As librarians, we have been trained to use resources and to assist others in their research. There are times, however, when we need to do our own research and hone our powers of observation. Many libraries keep a notebook with information about school assignments near the reference desk. Some of the information in such notebooks comes directly from teachers who communicate regularly with their librarians or faithfully send in completed assignment alert forms. Librarians are always grateful to those teachers, and the students in their classes have a much better chance of finding appropriate material and of making excellent use of the time spent doing research.

But what about students whose teachers are too busy to send in assignment alert forms or are not familiar with a library's resources and the research process? Instead of complaining about teachers' lack of preparation or knowledge, we should focus on how we can best meet students' information needs within the confines of the situation. Since public librarians often encounter confused students and parents working on assignments after school and on the weekends, I will offer a sample situation and suggest some responses.

Sample Reference Interview with a Student

LIBRARIAN: Hi. May I help you?

STUDENT: I need to find some information about rocks.

LIBRARIAN: Are you looking for information about any particular kind of rock or just rocks in general?

STUDENT: I don't know.

LIBRARIAN: Do you need information for a rock collection or for school?

STUDENT: It's for school.

LIBRARIAN: What kind of rocks are you studying? Crystals? Minerals?

STUDENT: I don't know. She just wants us to do a project on rocks.

LIBRARIAN: What kind of project?

STUDENT: We need to choose a favorite rock, scan a colored picture of it, and write some stuff about it.

LIBRARIAN: Do you have a favorite rock?

STUDENT: Not really.

LIBRARIAN: Let me show you some general books about rocks. You can look through them, and then, when you choose a favorite one, let me know, and we'll find more information about it.

While the student is leafing through the nature guides on rocks, the librarian has many choices for follow-up. If the library is busy, the student will probably be left alone until he or she approaches the librarian with another question. But if the librarian has time, he or she may try the following follow-up procedure:

Place at least one rock guide on temporary reserve for patrons working on the same assignment.

With your assignment notebook in hand, gently approach the student and ask for the name of his or her school, grade, and teacher. Ask when the assignment is due and what types of resources the teacher has suggested the students use. Also ask if any other classes are working on the same assignment.

Look for some Web sites with pictures of rocks. Note site addresses in your notebook, as well as the titles of useful reference books.

E-mail the student's school librarian to see if he or she knows anything else about the assignment or can suggest other resources.

If several students are working on the assignment and each has a slightly different interpretation of it, you might want to e-mail or call the teacher to ask for clarification.

Depending on the student's age and library experience, he or she may be able to find more specialized information about the chosen rock. However, it is best to play it safe and check back with the student and assist with the next research step.

In general, students tend to offer the librarian less information than needed, and the librarian has to coax out the details. Parents may leap to their own conclusions about assignments, which may make their child's work more complicated than it needs to be. Of course, neither parents nor librarians should second-guess the teacher's directions. As librarians, we can make inferences about the requirements of an assignment based on our own observations and past experiences, but we definitely feel more confident when we speak to the teacher or read a printed assignment sheet. Although we need to be cautious not to determine what an assignment is until we know for sure, sometimes our inferences and observations are the only information we have at our disposal when assisting a student.

6 Research and the Process of Discovery

Although school librarians and public librarians have different emphases in their day-to-day work, we all share some of the same frustrations. When I interviewed public and school librarians for this book and asked them what the main tensions in their work were, almost all of them, in their own words, expressed the same idea: Patrons/students/teachers do not realize how long research takes, that is, if one is going to do good research. They do not recognize the steps in the process, and they are unaware of the decisions that can or need to be made at each step.

We live in a fast-paced world, and people want answers fast. Students think they can find everything on the Internet in a matter of seconds. They fail to evaluate resources and need to learn more about balancing the types of materials they use. Librarians, who feel they are partially social workers, want to help as much as they can and create shortcuts for their patrons. Although such methods are beneficial to finding information quickly, students (and other patrons) need to know more about the research process.

School librarians are concerned that some teachers are not aware of the research process themselves and, as a result, assign inappropriate work to their students. These teachers are following a curriculum and feel pressured to cover a certain amount of material each day. Students must finish assignments, get answers, and then go on to the next topic so that they can do well on standardized tests. There is not much time for methodically noticing the steps of the research process and assessing what should be done at each step. Students are negatively affected by this fast-paced mind-set, and they could discover so much if the process were slowed down.

LEARNING THE RESEARCH PROCESS

When I was in library school, assignments often required us to take close note of the research process. For our reference course, we were given a weekly list of questions that we needed to answer using materials in the reference section of the university library. If our papers consisted only of lists of answers to the questions, however, the assignment was considered incomplete. We were also expected to list the sources of our answers and describe the process we used to find them. Did we consult other sources first? Why was the information in those sources inadequate? How did we think to look in the next source? Did serendipity play a role? If so, did we just happen to glance at the right book on the shelf, or did other clues lead us to the right place? Maybe we weren't able to answer the question to our satisfaction. If that case, why did we stop looking when we did? What limitations existed? To what extent could we know something for sure? Which issues tended to have less specific, absolutely true information written about them than others?

For some questions, I found the notation of process annoying and unnecessary. If I knew the definition of a word, for example, why did I need to look it up? Couldn't I just claim prior knowledge? Besides, wasn't arriving at the answer the most important thing, regardless of how it was done? My patience wore thin as I wrote a step-by-step description of how and why I arrived at each answer to each question in an assignment. Yet, as my searches became more thorough and precise, I realized that much was to be discovered at each step of the way. The same word, for instance, may have different definitions in different dictionaries; as a consequence, the next source I selected to look at could depend on which definition I thought was best to use in that specific instance. After numerous steps, given that each step was based on the results I found and the choices I made in the prior steps, the possible answers could vary tremendously.

In another class, on library history, we were required to write a final research paper. And, as if it were not enough work to write the paper itself, we again had to write about our research process. How did we choose a topic for the paper? What early steps did we take to define our area of focus, to develop our argument? Which sources did we consult? How helpful were those sources? How reliable were they? How did we move on to the next group of sources? What information was discovered in unlikely places? Which paths did we choose not to follow and why? Which people did we talk to and in what context? How did we decide it was time to stop researching and start writing? After doing some writing, how did we determine we needed to do more research? Again, being forced to become conscious of the process and write a narrative of it made me impatient. Wasn't all of this intuitive? Why take the time to note each step and write about it?

After I graduated and began working full-time in a public library, I realized how important it was for a librarian to notice these steps, how crucial it was for a librarian to have this skill. When working at the reference desk, a librarian needs to be able to assess which step of the research process a patron is at and join him or her in taking the next step. The patron is most interested in the end product, a concrete answer. The librarian, on the other hand, steps back and asks, Is there a concrete answer to this question? What are some possible sources to check? Which source should we try first and why? Is this topic better researched on the Internet or in print resources?

TEACHING THE RESEARCH PROCESS

Teachers and students, as well as the general public, tend to be unfamiliar with research issues. How can we, both school and public librarians, help others become more aware of how research works? A brief list of suggestions follows.

1. In our interactions with teachers, we can talk about the research projects their students are working on and encourage them to acknowledge each step taken to complete a project. Deciding on a topic, investigating sources, brainstorming, taking notes, evaluating related Web sites—each of these can be its own assignment, acknowledged by teachers' comments and, if appropriate, a grade.

2. When assisting students, spend time talking with them to discover more about their assignments as well as how much interest they have in their topics.

3. Suggest that students and teachers read widely before focusing on one specific aspect of a topic.

4. If a student is interested in a topic, the entire process goes more smoothly. When possible, look for signs of a student's interest and build on them. A research project should begin in a loose and open state, with many potential directions for exploration. The student should have the right (within reason) to take the direction which most interests him or her.

5. Encourage comfort in the midst of chaos. Often, because people want an immediate answer, they are unable to cope with a temporary state of chaos; they want everything to be clear at every step of the way. In reality, research, like any creative activity, has its messy moments, and it is during such moments that new ideas and directions are often discovered.

6. Help students become more mindful of how and why they do their work. Ask guiding questions: Are you finding what you need? Where does your assignment stand at this moment? What have you found out so far? Was that source helpful? What questions did your source answer and what new questions did it raise for you? Which direction would you like to go in next? Many students will say they just want to finish their homework quickly so that they can play a computer game. But if you can engage some of the students some of the time, it will help in the long run.

7. If students are either apathetic or anxious about an assignment, try your best to be positive. Soothe any feelings of inadequacy by acknowledging that research is hard work. Then, offer hope by pointing out appropriate resources they may not have known about.

MOTIVATING LEARNERS

How can we get students excited about the research process? In many ways, it's similar to how we motivate them to read and love books for pleasure reading. In readers' advisory work, we try to figure out what patrons' interests are. We ask them what types of books they have liked in the past. Do they like mysteries, poetry, realistic fiction? Do they have any favorite authors or characters? What kinds of books do they dislike? Have they heard about any new books they might be interested in? Then we move on to the next step: we find books related to those they liked in the past; we build on their interests by starting with the familiar and moving, bit by bit, to the unfamiliar. Unless a reader is ready, we do not recommend something entirely different.

When recommending books for pleasure reading, we are usually able to find some titles to meet a patron's interests. When recommending books for a research project, however, our choices are more limited. The assignment may include restrictions that do not allow a student to pursue certain topics or aspects of topics that hold potential interest. Other assignments, such as the request that students read a biography of a person of their choice, are less restrictive. In such cases, we can both help students to fulfill their assignment and encourage them to pursue areas they enjoy investigating.

One other way to encourage excitement in the research process is to focus on discovery. There are many analogies to detectives and clues in library games and lessons because doing research is often seen as similar to solving a mystery. When working with students, we can model the same eagerness and curiosity a detective has when working on a case. For appropriate questions, finding the answer is very much an "Aha! We made a discovery!" type of process.

Other situations call for a less methodical, subtler approach. I often think of Jane Yolen's book *Owl Moon* as being about the process of discovery. There are no books or assignments in the story, but the search for experience and knowledge plays a major role in the plot. On one moonlit winter night, a girl and her father walk into the woods to search for an owl. Certain expectations must be met when looking for this owl: "If you go owling / you have to be quiet, / that's what Pa always says." Similarly, when one is doing research, a quiet moment can allow the space needed for thought and discovery. In addition to encouraging a quiet atmosphere, the father models information-seeking behavior: "He looked up, / as if searching the stars, / as if reading a map up there." The child watches and notes the father's actions, sensing their importance in the search for an owl. Parents, teachers, and librarians all need to recognize the significance of offering guidance as youth embark on the research process, especially when using Internet resources.

Other qualities reflected in Yolen's poem that are related to the research process include patience and persistence, most notably when the father calls for an owl and hopes for a return call:

> Again he called out.
> And then again.

> After each call
> he was silent
> and for a moment we both listened.
> But there was no answer.
> Pa shrugged
> And I shrugged.
> I was not disappointed.
> My brothers all said
> sometimes there's an owl
> and sometimes there isn't.

The father continues to call and search, never giving up hope. His child calmly follows along, realistically staying open to the possibility that they may not spot an owl on this particular evening.

Similarly, when we guide a student through the search in the online catalog and then through the stacks, we need to encourage patience, persistence, and openness to the possibility that the library may not have the exact materials the student wants. Sometimes a book about Henry Ford is available, and sometimes one isn't. Sometimes a book has been written about the newest discovery in astrophysics, and sometimes one hasn't been. But when a student finds just the information he or she has been looking for, enjoy the discovery with him or her—share the excitement over seeing the newest book about Saturn or koala families. Such moments are meant to have a touch of wonder about them; at the least, they can offer a feeling of relief that the information is available!

The final stages of the search process are beautifully expressed in *Owl Moon*. The setting for the owl sighting is a clearing in the dark woods:

> Then we came to a clearing
> in the dark woods.
> The moon was high above us.
> It seemed to fit
> exactly
> over the center of the clearing
> and the snow below it
> was whiter than the milk
> in a cereal bowl.

The narration, from the point of view of the child, expresses both wonder and familiarity. The child and her father have just exited a dark, heavily wooded area where the child had feared "black shadows" and unseen "kinds of things" hiding behind trees. The open space and moonlight offer a safer atmosphere that invites one in, offering feelings of relief and a moment of clarity. The child senses that something amazing could happen here, yet she also focuses on how the view relates to her familiar, everyday world: the snow, she says, "was whiter than the milk / in a cereal bowl." Finally, when a great horned owl is heard and then sighted, the father and child stand transfixed: "For one minute, / three minutes, / maybe even a hundred minutes, / we stared at each other."

Although many of our young patrons may not consider their search for materials in the library as amazing as the search for a great horned owl in the woods, I hope my comparison illustrates some of the emotional qualities that can accompany any search for knowledge and experience.

7 School Services at the Public Library

HELPING TEACHERS MAKE
THE MOST OF THE PUBLIC LIBRARY

The type and extent of services available for teachers varies widely from library to library. How much a public library serves its area schools depends on the extent to which it is needed. In areas with excellent school libraries, a public library will still need materials to support curriculum but will be able to focus on encouraging reading for pleasure and preschool programming. In locations where school libraries are very small or nonexistent, public libraries will need to provide even basic materials to use in the classroom. All public libraries, regardless of size, should consider offering teacher cards and a materials request service.

Teacher Cards

Special library cards are often available to teachers who work in a school located in the library's district. The teachers may or may not reside in the library district. The card is specifically intended for checking out materials to be used in the classroom. For all other items, teachers need to use their personal cards from their home libraries. The privileges accompanying teacher cards may include an extended lending time for materials or an automatic waiver of fines. Teachers should be held responsible for all materials checked out on their card, even if they choose to lend those materials to their students and colleagues.

Since classes tend to concentrate on a topic for more than a couple of weeks, the extended lending time can give teachers more flexibility in planning. In addition, the longer time period provides more students with the opportunity to use the materials. For example, if a library sends fifteen books on rain forest animals to a third-grade class, twenty to thirty students can each have easy access to all fifteen books for several weeks. Those students do not need to persuade their parents to take them to the library for rain forest resources, worry about overdue books, or risk going to the library and having all the rain forest books checked out. The rain forest books have gone to the place where they are needed most for the moment. If a classroom has that collection of books for a month or more, students will be able to delve more deeply into the material and have time to discuss the books with each other and their teacher. An extended check-out procedure can also lift some burden from the school library when several classes in one school are studying the same topic at the same time and extra copies of books are needed. Public and school librarians can also pull together to obtain extra copies through interlibrary loan. The check-out period will most likely be predetermined, however, by the lending library and normally cannot be changed.

Some teachers do, unfortunately, abuse the privileges of the teacher card system and keep books for an entire semester or longer. A library that prefers to issue individual teacher cards and does not want to use fines as a motivation for returning books can try the following options:

A teacher who has overdue or missing materials may not be allowed to check out any new materials.

Notices may be sent to a teacher stating that his or her borrowing privileges will be permanently suspended if materials are not returned.

As a last resort, the library director may write a letter to the principal of the teacher's school describing the situation and asking the principal to speak with the teacher.

Instead of issuing cards to individual teachers, some libraries offer school cards with stated policies regarding financial responsibility for library materials. Sometimes the school itself will be held responsible for the materials, and the principal signs an agreement stating that she or he will collect the money due and pay the library. A school may set up a fund to pay for lost or damaged library materials, or it may determine that teachers will pay for materials if they were the last to use them. Whichever option is chosen, the public library may have only one or two contact persons at a school (usually the school librarian and the principal). Those contact persons handle all circulation issues. The advantage of the school card system is that the public library can withhold schoolwide privileges until all books lent to that school are returned or paid for. Such a system encourages schools to resolve their circulation and missing item issues themselves. However, it can be unfair for individual teachers, who may lose access to public library materials for their classrooms until their colleagues return or pay for late or missing books.

Materials Request Service

In an ideal world, teachers would have plenty of preparation time to spend browsing in their school and public libraries, searching for the perfect resources for their classrooms. Yet, in reality, even librarians, for whom collection development and familiarity are top priorities, cannot stay current with the thousands of new titles that come out every year. Public librarians can, however, offer to gather materials for teachers based on specific requests and have them ready for pickup when the teacher arrives.

Often a request will need to be refined so that the librarian can find useful and appropriate material for the teacher and his or her students. Figure 7.1 shows a sample form that contains all the important questions a librarian needs to ask while speaking with a teacher. It provides space for basic information, notes on subject and material types, and a record of action taken.

Other useful information includes the following:

- Would you like fiction or nonfiction materials or both?
- Do you and your students have any favorite authors?
- How many books do you need?
- What kind of projects or assignments will the students use the materials for?
- Would books from the adult department be appropriate?
- Do you have students of widely differing reading levels?
- Would you like any of the materials in languages other than English?

FIGURE 7.1
Materials Request for Teachers Form

Ela Area Public Library District
275 Mohawk Trail, Lake Zurich, IL 60047

Ph. (847) 438-3433   Fax (847) 438-9290   www.eapl.org

Materials Request for Teachers

Date: _____

Teacher: _____

School: _____

Grade/Reading Level: _____

Pick Up ❑   Van Delivery ❑

Subject And Material Types:

_____

_____

_____

_____

_____

Date Needed By: _____

Action Taken

Number Of Items Sent: _____

Due Back: _____

Request Taken By: _____

For your own record keeping, it is wise to include specified sections on the form for the date the request was made, the date the teacher needs the material, the number of items selected and checked out on the teacher's card, and the date the materials are due back at the library. If you save the forms and evaluate them after a couple of years, you will begin to see patterns that will guide you in future collection development. Many teachers request the same things at the same time each year, so if you keep the forms with notes of the materials you found in a previous year's search, some new searches will be much easier.

A materials request service is convenient for teachers. By making a quick phone call or sending an e-mail message to the librarian, teachers can have just the right materials waiting for them when they drive by the library after school. In some areas, the public library or the school system has a delivery van that can transport materials back and forth between the public library and the school. Such service is even more convenient, but teachers may need to wait several days or a week if the van does not run daily. When that is the case, libraries can offer a choice: would you like to pick the materials up yourself or have them delivered by the van, which will most likely make its next trip to your school on Friday?

In schools with excellent libraries, teachers may not need to use a service such as the one just described. On the other hand, public librarians might find that teachers often need duplicate copies of books or a wider range of materials than those available at the school library. In any case, it is best to have teachers also check their school libraries. When teachers make direct requests to the public library and overlook the school library, everyone suffers. School librarians may lose contact with teachers and no longer know which materials are most needed by the school, and the public library may become overwhelmed with requests.

Public libraries establishing a materials request service for teachers will need to set up some basic guidelines. Those guidelines will vary depending on a library's particular situation. Larger libraries, for instance, may not need to place restrictions on the number of books provided to each teacher, whereas smaller libraries may have to set a limit. Establishing guidelines and then presenting them in a school services or teacher services brochure or handbook is helpful. The guidelines should include the length of the borrowing period, the possibility of renewal, the policy describing fines, the number of days needed to prepare materials, and who is eligible for the request service.

The last point can become complicated. Sometimes the geographic area a public library serves does not exactly correspond to the geographic area served by a school district. Some sections of a school district may be within the jurisdiction of one public library district while other sections may be within the service area of an entirely different library district that could have a different philosophy of serving schools. The teachers themselves may live in one library district or another and not even be aware of where their home public library is located. The boundaries of districts, townships, villages, and cities twist and turn and overlap and leave everyone confused. Unfortunately, we are still a long way from simplifying local government, ending geographical disputes, and calming angry taxpayers. We can, however, try to serve teachers and students as best we can by setting up clear guidelines and establishing cooperative arrangements with our neighboring public libraries.

PUBLIC LIBRARIES SERVING STUDENTS

Several decades have passed since what Don Sager termed the "blackboard curtain" collapsed (Sager 1997). As was discussed in chapter 1, population growth in the 1940s eventually led public libraries to limit their service to students during the 1950s, 1960s, and 1970s. Although a busy library has usually been seen as a good sign, librarians during that period were not able to meet the demands of so many new patrons and, as they became overwhelmed, created policies that would enable them to maintain some semblance of order during the after-school hours—that time period when a tremendous number of children and young adults came to do homework or simply hang around until their parents picked them up. The policies became increasingly restrictive, limiting the times students could use the library and requiring permission slips from teachers and parents to borrow materials. In her book *The Fair Garden and the Swarm of Beasts,* Margaret A. Edwards (1969) came to the defense of young adults and urged librarians to respect them. She stated, "As one high-school girl put it, the relation of a librarian to young adults should be that of a hostess to a house guest."

Public libraries gradually came to recognize that students were part of the community and that students' parents were the taxpayers funding libraries. In fulfilling their mission to serve *all* the population, public libraries acknowledged the importance of serving students. And, as both school and public libraries were more heavily used than ever before, it became more evident that public library programs for school-age children and youth did not curtail the development of school library media centers, as had previously been thought. As communities began to understand the interrelated missions and roles of libraries, schools, and other agencies, the public library started offering more formal learning support. Offering reference and homework assistance to children and young adults allowed the public library a chance to encourage that group of patrons to appreciate libraries, increase their information literacy skills, and participate in recreational and educational library-sponsored programs.

When the blackboard curtain fell, however, a certain amount of chaos followed, and libraries had to redefine their mission to students. That redefinition process has been ongoing. Working with students continues to be one of the most significant challenges public librarians face on a daily basis. First, how do librarians cope with the huge onslaught of questions after school? What about the noise level? How can anyone concentrate if there are so many people running through the stacks? What should we do if the middle-school students take over all fifty Internet stations? And they always find the X-rated sites, either intentionally or unintentionally, no matter what we do! What do we do if students are lying on the table, sleeping on the floor, giggling in the bathroom? And they sneak food and beverages in all the time! Call the library monitors! This isn't our job!

In addition to coping with behavior problems, what do we do about all those vague, mysterious, or overly difficult assignments students ask us to help them with? Don't they have a clue about what the library does and does not have? Don't their teachers know how to create a decent assignment? How much help does the teacher want us to give students? To what extent are students supposed to figure things out on their own? Should we help with homework questions over the phone? Is it ethical? Wouldn't it be poor service to refuse the information?

Establishing Sound Policies

Unfortunately, there are no easy answers to such questions, no quick antidote to our frustration. Each community needs to assess its situation and make decisions on homework assistance, computer use, and behavior in the public library. Reasonable but nonrestrictive policies may help calm the atmosphere down a level or two. Here are some issues to consider when creating policies:

> Consider hiring staff whose primary duty is to maintain an appropriately quiet and calm atmosphere. They should walk throughout the

library constantly during busy times, politely asking those who are too noisy to quiet down or move to a different area.

Have some designated quiet areas. Accept that there will be different noise levels in different sections of the library.

Come to a consensus about when it is appropriate to ask someone who has been misbehaving to leave (whether the person is a child or an adult).

Consider the consequences of suspending the "no food or drink" rule in the library. Would it make that much difference if you did allow food and drink? Everyone sneaks food in anyway. If there were no rule against it, you wouldn't have to inform people, constantly, that it isn't allowed. On the other hand, if you have elegantly designed furniture, you may want to consider limiting food and drink to one specified section of the library.

Place pencils and scrap paper on desks and tables and near your online catalog. You might even want to have a supply area with scissors, markers, tape, staplers, and notebook paper available for the public to use in the library.

Keep teachers informed about the library's collection and invite them to come for workshops.

Once policies and guidelines have been established, the library staff will need to meet occasionally to see if any changes should be made. Yet, no matter how much the staff tries to maintain an agreeable tone in the library, there will be times when patience wears thin. At those times, take comfort in the fact that a busy library *is* a sign of a healthy, dynamic community that cares about the education of its youth and lifelong learning.

Homework Centers

Many different motivations have led to the creation of homework centers in public libraries across the country. They range from a library's desire to focus and calm the energy of unattended, bored children hanging out at the library to meeting local mandates for providing after-school prevention programs for children and teens. When a space is specially designated for doing homework, librarians have found it easier to discipline children's behavior. Cindy Mediavilla (2001) claims that "the space itself defines the appropriate behaviors required to do homework, and so the library's rules of conduct are more easily enforced."

In addition to encouraging a calmer atmosphere in the library, homework centers are especially advantageous to students who do not receive scholastic support or help with homework at home. They can consult with others in the center to clarify a confusing assignment, or, in the best of situations, have access to a homework center volunteer, tutor, or paid staff member. English as a Second Language (ESL) students may especially need assistance, as their parents may have little knowledge of English. Homework assignments can be daunting to ESL students, and a bilingual tutor can greatly contribute to their scholastic success.

Staffing a homework center is a complex issue. Paid assistants tend to be much more reliable than volunteers, but few libraries can afford the luxury. Consequently, most centers depend on volunteers, ranging from high-school Honor Society students who are doing community service to local college students training to become teachers. In some communities, libraries and school districts work together to provide funding for paid tutors. In Westchester County, New York, under the direction of the Tall Tree Initiative, students receive homework assistance from local teachers employed part-time by the public library to work after-school hours. Many public libraries now offer students live homework help through Tutor.com, a service that connects each student to a tutor who provides one-on-one help. When a student logs on to the service, he or she designates a grade level and a subject area. The student is then matched with a tutor who is an expert in that area. The general public can access the service for an hourly rate of twenty-five to sixty dollars, but students with an ID and a password from a subscribed library have free access.

Even if your homework center is in the bare bones stage, you can still offer a place conducive to studying. If possible, set up your homework center in a location separated from the traffic path of preschoolers and their parents. Corner spots in the children's or young adult sections, with tables and nearby computers, are ideal locations. On shelving surrounding the area, many libraries provide copies of textbooks used in local schools, books set aside for special assignments, and basic reference materials. A supply cabinet can also be useful, complete with a compass, protractor, calculator, ruler, markers, crayons, scissors, and pencil sharpener. Bulletin boards can display copies of assignment-related tips and Web sites as well as posters describing programs of interest to children and teens. The library may also offer classes in the center to teach students computer skills and research techniques that will help them complete school assignments. Library-sponsored Web pages listing and describing sites useful for typical homework assignments should be kept up-to-date and made easily accessible on computers in the center. To extend school–public library collaboration even further, the library may promote book discussion groups focusing on novels being read in school. Overall, the homework center and its programs create more fluid boundaries between the missions of the schools and the public library and provide students with a more thorough, deeper educational experience.

Class Visits to the Public Library

Class visits provide one option to introduce the public library to students whose parents do not take them to the library. Once those students see the public library, they may ask their parents to drive them to the library frequently. Teachers also enjoy visiting the library with their classes and learn as much as their students do about the resources available to them.

Transportation to and from the public library can be a complicated issue. In many school districts, classes are allowed a set number of field trips per year. Teachers may prefer to use their one or two permitted bus trips for longer excursions and pass up the opportunity to go to the public library for a tour or program. In other school districts, students need to pay part of the transportation cost for field trips. Even though the cost is usually subsidized by the school district, some students cannot afford to pay the two- to three-dollar required fee. For this reason, teachers, especially those who have students from low-income families, may limit the number of field trips they offer to their students. Students from low-income families are the ones we most hope to introduce to the public library, and they are also the students whose parents are least likely to visit the library habitually. How do we approach this catch-22 situation?

Many libraries have found that if they provide the money for transportation, teachers enthusiastically sign their classes up for tours. One excellent way to use grant money is to pay for buses. After the grant runs out, one can approach the school district about possible funding that would pay for a set number of classes (such as all fourth grades) to visit the public library annually. Depending on the community, the funding could come from a variety of sources: school district and library funding, corporate sponsorship, or contributions from individuals.

Some schools, fortunately, are close enough to the public library for classes to walk over on a nice day. Encourage the teachers at those schools to bring their classes to the library for tours, book talks, and other programs. Since some teachers tend to show up unannounced with fifty students, kindly remind them to arrange their visit a week or several days ahead of time so that the public library can ensure adequate staffing to handle the large group. The circulation department will be particularly eager to know when a large group of patrons is expected.

School Visits

Since arranging transportation to the library proves cumbersome and expensive, many library districts have decided to send librarians to the schools to visit students in their classrooms. Visiting librarians provide a welcome break in the routine of the school day. During a librarian's visit, students begin to see him or her as part of their familiar, everyday world. Later, if the students visit the public library, they recognize one or two staff members and feel comfortable asking for help. In addition, if a librarian ends a classroom visit by expressing hope that the students will visit soon, the students will arrive at the public library anticipating a friendly greeting or conversation.

Public librarians tend to focus on reading as recreation and learning as an activity in which people choose to participate throughout their lives. Those giving classroom presentations must have a true love of books, research, and learning in order to spread enthusiasm naturally. This enthusiasm manifests itself in a wide variety of ways because librarians have differing philosophies and practices due to their individual training, experience, personality, resources, and location. If librarians take advantage of their personal talents and background, they will offer excellent presentations.

There is a certain degree of controversy about whether public librarians should visit classrooms or not. Some school librarians feel that the school building and its classrooms are within their professional jurisdiction and that public librarians doing outreach are stepping beyond their rightful territory. This attitude may be especially prevalent if the school librarian's job is in jeopardy or if the school librarian fears that the public librarian will promote more use of the public library and less use of the school library. Public librarians can encourage a school to welcome them with open arms by promoting library use *in general* and by suggesting that children use the school library while in school and the public library after school, on weekends, and in the summer.

If the school and public librarians do not communicate with each other on a regular basis, confusion may result over what each librarian is presenting to the classes. Some may worry that book talks are repeated, but this fear is totally unfounded. Even if two librarians prepare mystery book talks for fourth graders, the chance that they will both discuss the same books in the same way is minuscule. So many great books and topics exist, and each person reacts to information in an individual way; in general, the more book talks students listen to, the more likely they are to hear about a book they would like to read.

Other Services

A feeling of goodwill between the public library and area schools can lead to any number of cooperative efforts. Whenever possible, the two should help each other out. Schools and libraries can lend each other microphones, craft materials, costumes, parking spaces, and review journals. Such small favors go a long way toward fostering good relations and building a strong community.

Larger libraries offer services to schools that most of us can only dream about. The Multnomah County Library in Oregon has a School Corps made up of several staff members. The corps offers many electronic resource workshops for classes, customized book lists and webliographies, presentations on censorship, book talks on any topic requested, and many other amazing programs for students, parents, and families. To find out more and become inspired, check out their Web site at www.multnomah. lib.or.us/lib.

Most of all, we need to offer our fellow librarians at other institutions emotional and professional support, especially when intellectual freedom issues arise. Support is also welcome during transitions, whether that transition be a move from one library building to another, a major change in technology, or adapting to the evolving role of library service in the community.

8 A Day in the Life

Too often, and especially during hectic times, we imagine that our colleagues at other institutions have easier jobs and spend their days sitting around, polishing their toenails. The truth is that we are all working very hard, and we each have different joys and struggles depending on our individual situations. I hope the personal narratives in this section will lend some levity to the conflicts and also give you a sense of what it is like to walk in another librarian's shoes.

NATALIE ZIARNIK

7:55 A.M. While balancing several books, my lunch, and my traveler's mug of coffee, I struggle to punch in the entry code at the back door to the library. A few books fall as I open the heavy door, and I rush into the staff room and drop all my stuff on a chair. After placing my lunch in the refrigerator, I gather my things and enter the Technical Services Department. Many of the technical services staff are morning people and are already bustling about, cheerful and alert. As I pass through the department, someone might give me a package containing items I ordered for a program, ask for cataloging information on a French language book, or offer a warm chocolate chip cookie. Some days I linger a few minutes and listen to stories about staff members' children, informally picking up information about teachers, assignments, activities, or problems in the schools. But today I can't stay. Too much awaits me in my office.

8:05 A.M.   The sound of a vacuum cleaner sucking up bits of candy in a far corner echoes through the dark Children's Services Department. Our maintenance crew strives to save electricity and often works in near darkness. I turn on the lights to find the way to my office, even though maintenance will turn them back off in a couple of minutes. After switching on my computer, I water the plants, check my inbox for notes and requests from teachers and staff, and then notice that three voice-mail messages are waiting:

1. "Hello. This is Cynthia Merck. I teach third grade at Quentin. We're doing a unit on fairy tales, and I noticed from your brochure that you're offering a Little Red Riding Hood program. Could you come to our class next Thursday at . . . about 9:40 in the morning? Or tomorrow, Thursday, would be fine, too. Actually any Thursday this month. But it pretty much has to be at 9:40. Two of the other third-grade teachers would like you to come, too. Do you want to come on the same day for all of us? Give me a call. Thanks."

2. "Hi, Natalie. Susan over at St. Francis here. New social studies textbooks just arrived. Saved you some. Could we get together at 11:00 tomorrow to go through those old St. Francis textbooks on the shelves and see which ones we don't need anymore? We're sending a load of used textbooks to inner-city schools next week. Again, it's Susan at 791-4582. Talk to you later."

3. "Hi. It's Kathleen. Maybe you've already thought about this, but I thought I'd call and check just in case. What kind of room setup do you need for your brown-bag talk next Tuesday? I was talking with Linda and she wondered if you needed a laptop or a screen or projector. Also, let me know if you were able to contact the person to make the cake. Thanks, Natalie."

Meanwhile, e-mail messages are piling up in my computer's inbox. A teacher has requested thirty books on the solar system for her second-grade class. Another teacher writes that she received an overdue notice for a book she is certain she returned last month. A fourth-grade teacher wants me to give a book talk on mysteries in three weeks. A school librarian needs some of our books about careers to supplement her library's collection for the duration of an assignment.

I return as many calls and e-mails as possible before nine o'clock. My basket containing puppets and picture-book versions of Little Red Riding Hood tales is all prepared. Barb, our crafts expert in the department, has encouraged me to wear an overly cute Little Red Riding Hood costume for my school visits, but I do not feel up to the challenge. My red fall coat and the basket will act as sufficient costume. Just as I'm prepared to leave, I grab some activity handouts to give to the classes. I count the handouts; I'm about sixty short. Not again! I rush into the graphics room and ask for help printing and folding brochures.

9:27 A.M.   As I head out the door, I tell the staff at the information desk that I will be out of the building, at Sarah Adams School, for about two and a half hours. They say, "Fine, see you later, Little Red!"

9:32 A.M.   I'm two minutes late for a class visit, but I'm not worried about it. The teachers at Sarah Adams are usually pretty laid back and appreciative no matter what. When I'm scheduled to visit Isaac Fox School, however, I arrive precisely five minutes early. If I don't, the teachers will call the library and wonder if I forgot to come or had a traffic accident. To an outsider, each school provides an opportunity to learn about and adapt to a new miniculture.

After I press the school's security doorbell, the secretary peeks through the window at me and smiles. "Urrrpt," the security system blurts out, and I push the door and gain entrance. After signing in at the desk, I put a visitor sticker on my dress as the secretary alerts the classroom teacher of my arrival.

This school secretary stays current. She knows whose classrooms I'm visiting, what time I'm supposed to be at each one, and whether any teachers are sick, have student teachers, or are off schedule for one reason or another. She's even up-to-date on which teachers have lost a library book or two. Her memory is incredible, as she will remember which classrooms I've frequently visited and which ones I visit so rarely that I get lost in the hallways looking for the right room.

9:37 A.M. As I approach and enter the first classroom on my list, I hear children whispering to each other, "The library lady is here." "It's Natalie." "No, it's Mrs. Z." "It's the one who taught us string stories last year!" The teacher is busy in a far corner helping a group of students, so I put my basket down, take off my coat, get settled, and spend a few minutes chatting with the students. I recognize about half of them because they live near the public library and visit after school. A boy spots a stuffed wolf in my basket and asks to hold it. I'd like to give it to him, but through experience, I've learned that it's best to wait until after the program. Otherwise, the entire class will become distracted by whose turn it is to hold the wolf.

Finally, the teacher notices that I'm here. She rushes over with a big smile, asks me if I'm ready or if I need anything, and then calms the class down. This particular teacher, Mrs. Bronfield, tends to introduce me by connecting my presentation topic to the students' current schoolwork. She does it in a cheerful, enthusiastic way, so I don't feel that the students' attention to my talk is a curricular requirement. Other teachers just say, "Mrs. Ziarnik from Ela is here. Show her your best behavior." And then there are one or two who introduce me as the local children's literature expert.

Most class visits go smoothly, but a couple of teachers who invite me do not seem pleased when I arrive: "We're too busy today. Half the class failed the spelling test. Everyone needs to be memorizing their words now." "I forgot that we have a field trip today. Will your presentation take more than ten minutes?" "I really have to go to the bathroom and have a coffee break. Could you just take over? They're a little wild today, but they might settle down." "Next time I'd prefer that you stick with Aesop's fables. I'm not into this multicultural stuff."

9:45 A.M.   I begin by telling the story of Little Red Riding Hood, using puppets to tell short segments and asking for contributions from the class. At the story's end, we talk about different Little Red Riding Hood stories we've heard. Some kids make up their own details. If the class is focused enough, like this one is, I choose volunteers to act out the story using puppets. Afterwards, I read *Lon Po Po,* by Ed Young (1989), and *Petite Rouge: A Cajun Red Riding Hood,* by Mike Artell (2001).

We talk about the stories as long as the teacher will allow. The kids love the last version the best. The dialect must be the appealing aspect; so many students say, "I loved that language!" "That sound was so cool!" "How did you learn to talk like that?" I tell them we have several copies of the book at the public library so they can come after school to get a copy and practice reading aloud. The school library has one copy, and the teacher offers to check it out and bring it to class.

10:40 A.M.   I was due at the next class five minutes ago, so I quickly pass out handouts and explain the mandala coloring activity. After I encourage the kids to visit me at the library, I say a quick good-bye and rush down the hallway. A quiet class, each student with a cleared desk, awaits me.

11:25 A.M.   The preceding class was so quiet that the program went quickly and I have time to get a glass of water in the teachers' lounge. Baby pictures of the teachers fill the lounge's bulletin board, and there's a sign asking everyone to match each baby picture to a teacher's name. I don't recognize any of them until I see what others have guessed and then the babies' eyes and smiles start to look familiar. The principal, who is fairly new, comes in for coffee and asks me how summer reading went. He invites me to give a short talk on how parents of first graders can help their children learn to read. It's for a meeting next month, on a Tuesday evening. The first-grade team will be presenting the curriculum for first grade, and the principal was hoping the reading specialist and I could emphasize tips for parents, encourage use of the library, and promote reading for fun. I tell him I'd be glad to and promise to call tomorrow to confirm.

11:45 A.M. My final visit for the day begins. The class looks sleepy because they've just had lunch. My stomach is growling and I can't wait to get back to the library to eat. At the end of the program, as I'm preparing to leave, the teacher stops me and asks me to send her twenty-five biographies on "people who have made a difference." We talk for a few minutes to refine what that description really means.

12:30 P.M. I'm ready to go, but my coat has disappeared. I trace my steps and find it in the first classroom I visited in the morning. I'm known for inadvertently leaving a trail of items as I move from class to class, so no one is surprised to see me back again. As I pick up my coat, several students come up to me and present their decorated Little Red Riding Hood mandalas. Each student has taken a different approach, and the designs that were once identical now have separate tones, both in color and in emotion; how can students create such individual visions out of the same simple structure?

12:45 P.M. On my way out, I pass the school library and peek in to see if Caroline is free to talk, but she's busy teaching, as usual. This is Caroline's first year working in the library. She was a fourth-grade teacher at another school in the district for several years and enjoyed the children's literature aspect of her job so much that she decided to give school librarianship a try. Even though she does not yet have her library degree, all of us at the public library were relieved that she was offered the job. School librarians interested in children's literature make great colleagues for us, especially when we're working on collaborative projects such as Battle of the Books. From what we public librarians observe, many of the school librarians in our area choose or are forced to focus on technology instead of literature. Few school librarians have found a way to balance the time and energy spent on technology with that spent on literature and reading, but we are lucky enough to have a couple of them in our district.

12:46 P.M.   I sign out in the school office and head back to the Ela Library for lunch!

12:56 P.M.   Before eating, I call the information desk and my department to let them know that I'm back "home." I leaf through the local paper and notice that the fifth grades are doing projects on immigrants and their diaries. The artcle describes some students who have old diaries from their relatives who came to the United States last century; other students who are recent immigrants are presenting sections from their own diaries; and the newspaper suggests that more diaries and information can be found at the local library! I wonder how much material we have on that topic and intend to do a search after lunch.

1:20 P.M.   "Natalie, you'll never guess who called while you were out," Pam says as I enter the children's department. She has that look on her face, alerting me that one of *those* teachers has some issue or other. I guess a couple of likely suspects and finally guess correctly: "Violet Shark?"

"Yep," Pam says. "I always get the strange calls. Violet called and said that she is positive that she returned the book she just got an overdue notice for. She remembers dropping it off a couple of weeks ago."

"She sent me an e-mail about that this morning," I say, "and I wrote her and told her not to worry about it until I looked around for it."

"Well," says Pam, "she is worried, let me tell you. I guess she expected you to do the search first thing this morning. Like we don't have anything else to do around here! And the lost book isn't all. She wants you to find a children's literature conference going on in New Mexico that she can attend during her winter break."

"What? Why?" I ask.

"If there's a conference, the school will pay for her transportation, so she gets a free trip out to see her sister," Barb explains.

"Are you kidding?" I ask.

Barb shakes her head while she punches out fall leaves on the Ellison machine.

2:00 P.M.   I've assembled bags of books for the teachers who made requests this morning, one bag each with books on the solar system and mysteries, and two bags of biographies of "people who have made a difference." I take the bags to the circulation desk to see if the staff there has time to check the books out with a modern scanner and, thank goodness, they do. The teachers like the books to be checked out with the new system because it produces a printed receipt listing all the items checked out to the teacher's card. A couple of months ago, before this system existed, I checked out each book by hand, typing in the bar code numbers. A slip specifying how many items were checked out and when they would be due was attached to each book bag, but teachers were not given an itemized list. When they assembled the books to be returned to the library, often one or two would be missing, and the teachers didn't know which ones until we checked our records on the library's computer. It was a hassle, and I'm grateful to technology for the receipt printers.

2:35 P.M.   Boys dressed in navy pants and white shirts and girls wearing navy plaid jumpers with white blouses descend on the children's department like a flock of noisy blue jays. The kids are everywhere: in the computer rooms, lined up at the reference desk hoping to reserve the coveted study room, in the bathrooms giggling, or in the corners of the library rushing around to claim their favorite tables. St. Francis School is Ela Library's neighbor, and the library is the favorite hang-out spot for St. Francis students, with or without their parents. Here is a rundown of a typical after-school period on the reference desk:

2:36 P.M.   Taylor signs up for computer room 1.

2:38 P.M.   Taylor's computer freezes.

2:39 P.M.   Taylor's brother no longer wants to watch her play Barbie's Magic Hair Styler. He signs up for computer 2 and plays Lego Racers.

2:42 P.M.   A mother with one school-age girl of about seven years and two preschoolers leads her children over to the picture-book area.

2:47 P.M.   The mother goes downstairs, leaving her kids behind.

2:50 P.M.   The seven-year-old approaches the reference desk and asks for books on how snakes shed their skin.

2:52 P.M.   Taylor's computer freezes again.

2:53 P.M.   A group of three girls in blue plaid ask for help finding books on African American female aviators for their biography project. They are disappointed because we have only one book available on Bessie Coleman and it's only fifty-four pages long. They each need three sources and at least one biography of at least one hundred pages. I continue to search on the computer for possible interlibrary loan material.

2:55 P.M.   The seven-year-old dumps the book on snakes in the returns basket, browses in the Junie B. Jones section, chooses a book, and sits down to read, far from her younger siblings.

3:00 P.M.   A preschooler in the picture-book section is screaming, "Mommmmmy! Where are you?"

3:02 P.M.   We go on a search for the mother. She is downstairs, reading *Psychology Today* in the adult section, sitting comfortably in a big chair with her shoes off, legs curled underneath her. She gives me and her crying child blank stares.

3:07 P.M.   Quiet. I begin reading *The House on Hackman's Hill,* by Joan Lowery Nixon (1985), for an upcoming book talk on mysteries. A student stops by the reference desk and tells me she's read the book and that it was one of her favorites. I smile and ask her not to tell me too much about it so the ending won't be spoiled. She asks me if I'm going to be visiting her class soon, so I get my calendar and look it up. When I tell her that I'm visiting next week, she says "Yes!" and runs over to tell her friends.

3:12 P.M.   Rudolfo asks if there are any Homework Helpers in today. I look in the binder. "Sorry, not today," I say. Rudolfo, who is still struggling with English, could use a tutor, or at the very least, a high-school-volunteer Homework Helper, every day of the week. We've had trouble attracting a committed group of volunteers.

3:15 P.M.   Rudolfo asks me to explain the meaning of a story problem for his math class. He is persistent. Every day, he asks us librarians several homework questions—about math, reading, and especially vocabulary. When he looks up a word in the dictionary, he usually does not understand one or two words used in the definition. Rudolfo is consistently cheerful, but a little sneaky in a humorous way. We have to be careful that we help him find the answers himself and avoid giving in and doing his homework for him.

The day Rudolfo got his library card is one of my best recent library memories. He was having trouble reading *From the Mixed-up Files of Mrs. Basil E. Frankweiler,* by E. L. Konigsburg (1967), and I suggested that he check out the audiotape version to listen to as he read the book. He said he didn't have a library card and I asked, "Why not?" He mumbled something about his father being afraid to apply for one. I said that it was free, that all he needed was some mail to show where he lived, and that we would keep the card private—the government and police would know nothing about it. Rudolfo quickly left the library and came back just five minutes later with his father. I sent them down to get cards and moments later,

Rudolfo was up to get the audiotape as well as the video version of *From the Mixed-up Files.* His face radiated joy as he showed me the large pile of materials he was checking out to take home.

I've become so concerned about Rudolfo that I've telephoned his teacher to talk more about his language skills and have asked the assistant superintendent about setting up tutoring either at the library or at the schools for after-school ESL tutoring. We are making some progress in these areas but have a long way to go.

3:30 P.M.   And so the afternoon continues, with more computer troubleshooting, requests for books on nocturnal animals, questions about how to look up obscure people on the Internet, searches for the most recent Sailor Moon video, and numerous requests for books on "people who have made a difference," all from students in the class I visited earlier today—the one whose teacher requested that I send books to her classroom. What I'm wondering is, If I'm going to send these books to her classroom, why are the students here already getting their own copies? Some teachers, such as this one, are overly zealous about getting enough materials. Others are unaware of our collection's limitations and possibilities.

4:45 P.M.   A mother complains that our copy of the fourth-grade math textbook is missing just the pages her son needs. I call the school administration center and leave a message, asking for either another copy of the textbook or a photocopied set of the pages we are missing.

4:47 P.M.   A student comes in and says, "Hey, you came to my class today!" She wants to write her name on a small green paper tree. After she's done writing, I staple it up on the Little Red Riding Hood bulletin board, in the forest, underneath a large tree bearing the name of her teacher. She's the first one in her class to come to the library since my visit. She's excited that we still have a version of *Petite Rouge* available for checkout. After I find a copy for her, I quickly collect other versions of the tale to save for the

	display case. Tomorrow morning I have no class visits, so it will be a good day to put together a small exhibit.
5:05 P.M.	I check my e-mail one more time, decide that responses to the messages can wait until tomorrow, and head home.
8:10 P.M.	My three-year-old son wants me to tell him the story of Little Red Riding Hood.
2:30 a.m.	I wake up and notice that I have been dreaming about wolves in the forest.

Natalie Ziarnik is the Elementary School Liaison Librarian for the Ela Area Public Library District, Lake Zurich, Illinois.

PENNY MANDZIARA

A typical morning in my life as a library/school liaison starts around 8:00 A.M., with meetings in the various schools I serve. Our meeting topics range from deciding the scope and sequence of the curriculum and how library materials will fit in, to my role as a lead trainer in a mentoring program for eighth graders, to making a schedule of book-talking engagements. (I work as my own agent!)

As school starts, I may be found in a first-grade class in my frog costume, reading aloud *Frog and Toad Are Friends,* by Arnold Lobel (1970). After lunch, I will be wearing the same costume, this time introducing the new animal unit and reading Gail Gibbons's *Frog* (1993). In between, I visit classrooms to present book talks, promoting the Rebecca Caudill Young Readers' Book Award throughout the school. I also might pop into classrooms to read poems to the students for a poetry break.

I love to use costumes and props when I present a book talk. This seems to work surprisingly well with middle-school students. I wonder if students are just so shocked to see a middle-aged woman making a fool of herself.

I hardly ever experience students with behavior problems. I do not have any papers to grade, no parent-teacher conferences to attend. My sole purpose is to promote reading. In short, *I have the best job in the world!*

My afternoons are spent pulling together books, costumes, and props for the next day. I read about ten to twelve young adult novels a week and, no, I do not read at work! I sometimes take a turn at the reference desk, but at 3:45 P.M. our focus changes. This is the dismissal time for the middle school, right next door! We have a teen center that is open Monday through Thursday from 3:45 P.M. to 5:30 P.M. where staff take turns "hanging out" in "teen town." The program has been a great success.

I try to be involved in as many extracurricular activities in the school district as I can. I feel it is important for students to see me outside the library. Students also respond to a familiar face when they come back to the library. I might be running lines with student actors, providing leadership training to students involved in student council, or passing out popcorn at a PTA function. These practices benefit the library, but I also come away from each activity having had personal interaction with the students in my community. I hope they learn from me the importance of reading and a desire to become lifelong learners.

Every day at my job is different. Every year brings new costumes, new students, new books, and new opportunities to satisfy and delight my patrons. Like I said before: I have the best job in the world!

Penny Mandziara is a library/school liaison for the
Bensenville Community Public Library in Bensenville, Illinois.

CYNTHIA OAKES AND LORETTA M. GAFFNEY

7:30 A.M.	Open library and turn on lights.
	Greet library assistants and library technical assistant.
	Deal with security issues: doors and computer applications found open. Yikes!
	Four students enter. One has problems opening a file on disk. Deal with this for forty-five minutes while simultaneously . . .
7:45 A.M.	High-school and middle-school students start trickling in to study, read e-mail, find books to read, socialize, read e-mail.
	Ask them to be quiet.
	Readers' advisory . . . funny books, scary books, sad books, fantasy.

Help student find "green book" desperately needed for bibliography.

Look for open time slot so teacher can bring class in to do research today; no time available, completely booked.

Appease teacher.

8:00 A.M.   Check schedule with colleague to determine what we are supposed to be doing today.

Moment of panic.

Get coffee.

Joke around with coworkers.

8:15 A.M.   Prepare for fifth-grade small-group discussion on Lois Lowry's *The Giver* (1993).

8:30 A.M.   Explain the meaning of the term "stirrings."

Show a variety of colored paper sheets—students give emotional responses.

Hotly debate whether pink is a girl's color.

Get blown away by profound student interpretations of the power of color and sound in our world.

9:10 A.M.   Write late passes for students delayed by an exciting discussion that extended into next period—librarians are lousy at cutting off student-driven discussions.

Welcome impatient seventh graders and teacher waiting outside classroom door.

Appease teacher.

9:15 A.M.   Introduce seventh-grade students to print resources for upcoming research project on Salem witch trials.

Move to Feitler Computer Lab.

9:30 A.M.   Introduce same students to online resources, including online catalog, online encyclopedia, online magazine database, and Web resources selected, annotated, and placed on library Web page.

Explain why typing www.witches.com is not a good idea.

9:45 A.M.   Fifteen-minute student break.

Perform readers' advisory while simultaneously handing out passes for upcoming tutorial.

	Troubleshoot stubborn computer that will not print out student paper that was due yesterday.
	Appease student.
10:00 A.M.	Tutorial.
	Collect student passes as students sit down to study, research, read, socialize.
	Ask them to be quiet.
	Troubleshoot same stubborn computer; call library technical assistant for HELP.
	Assist with research projects on biotechnology, Salem witch trials, Chicago World's Colombian Exposition.
	Hand copy of *Eat Your Genes,* by Stephen Nottingham (1998), to student researching Anne Hutchinson.
	Talk with student about upcoming Bas Mitzvah and latest book by Tamora Pierce.
10:47 A.M.	Repeat introduction to Salem witch trials with new group of students.
	Forget to remind them why typing in www.witches.com is not a good idea.
	Moment of panic.
11:30 A.M.	Middle-school lunch.
	Spend fifteen minutes reminding students they can't come into the library for the next fifteen minutes—lunch is important, too.
	Share bag of cookies with student while reminding him he can't eat in the library.
	Laugh while same student reads a passage from a Daniel Pinkwater novel.
11:45 A.M.	Inhale lunch.
	Check e-mail, no time to respond.
12:00 P.M.	Attend grade-level meeting.
	Schedule next round of book talks with supportive teachers.
	Participate in planning upcoming field trip.
	Joke around with teachers.

12:45 P.M.	Meet with principal to discuss the possibility of reassigning librarian grade-level responsibility.
	Remember that the principal is your pal.
12:55 P.M.	Welcome regularly scheduled fifth-grade class.
	Read quietly together (librarian breathes).
	Introduce this year's Zena Sutherland Award nominees.*
	Readers' advisory . . . find funny books, sad books, mysteries, a "really, really good book."
1:45 P.M	Meet sixth-grade Zena Sutherland Award Committee.**
	Go to fourth-grade classes and take digital pictures while sixth graders introduce this year's Zena Sutherland Award nominees.
	Hug sixth graders and tell them they are AWESOME!
2:30 P.M.	Respond to e-mail.
	Open snail mail.
	Glance at schedule with colleague to determine what we are supposed to be doing tomorrow.
	Moment of panic.
	Squeeze in cataloging of materials needed next day.
	Work on Web page for tomorrow's research project.
	Quickly pull books for tomorrow's book talk.
3:30 P.M.	Get coffee.
	Joke around with colleagues and thank library assistants and technical assistant for handling overdues, processing books on the fly, fixing computers, fixing printers, changing toner in the copier, printing out bookmarks, checking out over two hundred books, copying last-

---

* The Zena Sutherland Award is given every year by the third- through fifth-grade students of the University of Chicago Lab Schools to the best picture book of the previous year.

** The Zena Sutherland Award Committee selects the nominated titles.

minute Web-page-evaluation sheets, and—most of all—appeasing librarians.

4:00 P.M.   Urge students still in library to enjoy the unseasonably warm weather by going outside.

Close and lock Feitler Lab.

Set alarm.

Grab new Tamora Pierce book to read overnight.

Turn out lights.

Lock doors.

Go home happy.

Cynthia Oakes and Loretta M. Gaffney are school librarians at the University of Chicago Laboratory Schools in Chicago, Illinois.

9 At the Potter's Wheel

While compiling information for this chapter, I was also reading *A Single Shard,* the 2002 Newbery Award winner by Linda Sue Park (2001). The story takes place in a potters' village in twelfth-century Korea. The main character, a thirteen-year-old orphan boy named Tree-ear, hopes to become a potter someday. In the opening chapters, Tree-ear hides behind the low branches of a tree, sneaking peeks at Min, a master potter, working at his wheel, throwing clay and transforming it into graceful vases.

Several aspects about creating pottery reminded me of how we create library and reading promotion programs. Like Tree-ear watching Min, we peek in during our colleagues' story times and book talks at work, hoping to learn new techniques. Although we do not observe secretively, we may not be as forthright as we could be about sharing ideas with other librarians and teachers in our communities.

In a later chapter of *A Single Shard,* the King's emissary plans a visit to Tree-ear's village to survey the work of the potters and choose one for a royal commission. Every potter prepares examples of his best work to display in a stall at the marketplace. Before the time of this public display, any new techniques are seen as private property and are not to be stolen by other potters. Yet, during the display, potters are free to visit one another's stalls and learn about new techniques to incorporate into their own work. In the words of Crane-man, Tree-ear's unofficial guardian and moral mentor, "once a man has revealed his ideas to others, it is no longer his alone. It belongs to the world."

Min, however, does not venture forth to observe the new inlay technique created by Kang, an inventive potter who lacks Min's patience, attention to detail, and overall skill. As the village's best potter, Min may be too proud to observe another's technique, or he may feel resentful because Kang made a notable discovery. Min continues to create traditional pots, working constantly and in silence to hide his frustration. Yet as soon as Tree-ear tells him about the inlay technique, Min immediately sets to work on it, taking aspects of Kang's idea and blending them with his own to create vases that "both honor tradition and welcome the new in a way that was worthy of a commission."

I hope the descriptions of the programs in this chapter will inspire you as Min was inspired. Please take whichever aspects are useful to you and blend them with the ideas and techniques that have worked for you in the past. Most of these programs are designed to promote reading for pleasure, with schools and the public libraries working together. A few programs are intended explicitly to encourage cross-institutional communication; others focus on research skills. No matter which you choose to mold to your individual situation, I hope you will share not only expertise and resources but also the entire programming experience with your local colleagues. May none of us—whether young or old or inexperienced or retired—be too proud or hesitant to incorporate others' ideas into our work or share our own. The potter's wheel and clay are ready for you. Take the materials and have fun!

AUTHOR OR ILLUSTRATOR VISIT

Cooperating Parties

Public and school librarians, teachers, bookstore managers, parent volunteers.

Level

All ages.

Program Description

An author or illustrator is invited to speak at area school(s) and the public library. The visit may last only a few hours or several days. Some schools and libraries have even had resident authors or illustrators who have stayed and worked for many months, providing in-depth workshops on the arts for local children. Authors are expensive and often charge more than a public library or school alone can afford, yet these authors are usually willing to arrange their schedules so that agencies can work together to afford them. The author may visit a school during the day, for example, and then give a talk at the public library in the evening. Although the author may charge for both programs, the school and library can split the cost of transportation and lodging.

Planning Tips

This program may be initiated by a wide variety of people, including a public or school librarian, bookstore manager, or teacher. The person initiating the program may already have a particular author or illustrator in mind or may be interested in having visitors in general. In either case, when approaching other individuals and agencies to participate and help out financially, offer everyone involved several options: Are they interested in this particular author or illustrator? Would they be willing to help pay for transportation and lodging? Could they offer a space for a talk or a book signing? Would someone be willing to pick up the author at the airport or take him or her to lunch?

If your potential partner is not interested in the chosen author, consider meeting at a future time to brainstorm for names of individuals you are both interested in inviting to the community.

Determine how much money you have to fund the event. You will need to budget money for the speaker's honorarium, travel, lodging, and food.

Contact the speaker either via e-mail or through his or her publisher.

Arrange a contract with the speaker. Include a firm appearance date, bad weather date, appearance times, price, and type and length of visit.

Publicize your event through the newspaper, school and public library newsletters, and posters.

Prepare students early so that they will be familiar with the speaker's work before the visit. Arrange displays of books in both the school and the public libraries. Rotate a collection of the author's work from classroom to classroom. Read a story written or illustrated by the speaker at story time.

Send the speaker a schedule before he or she arrives. The schedule should include flight times, names of people who might pick him or her up at the airport, class visit times, breaks, lunches, and a list of contact people.

Ask the speaker what kind of equipment he or she might need.

Provide the speaker with a glass of water at all times.

Expected Outcomes

Students become enthusiastic about an author's or illustrator's work.

Students' awareness of authors and illustrators as "real people" increases.

Students begin to understand the connection between art and life.

Students are introduced to the creative process.

Authors and illustrators often motivate students to create their own stories and art.

Libraries are given the opportunity to highlight areas of their collection.

Resources

The Internet is an excellent source for finding information about authors and their availability for visits. If you are looking for a local author, ask bookstores in the area for suggestions.

BATTLE OF THE BOOKS

Cooperating Parties

School and public librarians, teachers of grades 4 and 5, parent volunteers.

Level

Grades 4 and 5, but can be altered for other grade levels.

Program Description

Although many variations of this program exist, nearly all involve having students read books from a specified list, form teams, and compete in battles similar in format to *Scholastic Bowl* or *College Bowl*. In the Ela Area Public Library's program, readers form teams consisting of four or five members who all attend the same school. Players read books from a list of forty titles selected by the public library's children's department. During competition, the teams earn points by answering questions about those books.

The preliminary battles take place at the elementary schools and are usually administered by the school librarian and one or two teachers. The top two teams from each school are eligible for the second round of battles at the public library. Those teams each battle twice. From that group, the first-, second-, third-, and fourth-place teams compete in a final Grand Battle to determine the champions. The librarians bring a special treat to the winning team members during the school's lunchtime and present the winners with the Battle of the Books trophy, which will be housed at the winners' school until next year's Grand Battle. Each member of each team in the Grand Battle receives a gift certificate to a local bookstore.

Planning Tips

When selecting titles for the reading list, include books from a variety of genres.

If your state has a young reader's award, try to include as many of those titles as are appropriate.

Select books available in paperback to keep costs down. You will want to order multiple copies of each title.

Offer a "boot camp" for parents of children participating in the Battle for the first time.

Shelve the books on the Battle list in a special, easily accessible section of the library.

If possible, purchase a complete set of Battle books for the libraries of each participating school.

Keep Battle questions hidden in a secure place.

Warning: The Battle of the Books becomes more competitive and intense in subsequent years.

Expected Outcomes

Students read a wide selection of quality youth literature and become familiar with different genres and authors.

A community of readers forms; team members talk about books with each other as well as with members from other teams.

Students who attend different schools become acquainted with each other.

Public librarians, school librarians, and classroom teachers communicate and collaborate to provide a fair, exciting, and challenging Battle of the Books.

Teachers learn more about current youth literature. The titles on the yearly Battle of the Books lists often become well known in the classroom and are adopted into the curriculum.

Resource

Cook, Sybilla, Frances Corcoran, and Beverley Fonnesbeck. 2001. *Battle of the Books and More: Reading Activities for Middle School Students.* Fort Atkinson, Wis.: Alleyside.

Source: Pam Allen and Brenda Duff, Ela Area Public Library District, Lake Zurich, Illinois.

CAREER ADVISORY COUNCIL

Cooperating Parties

Local businesspeople; school faculty, including high-school teachers and librarians; public librarians; professionals representing various occupations and trades.

Level

Grades 9 through 12.

Program Description

The Career Advisory Council members promote a better understanding of career opportunities by providing students with support and guidance. The council meets monthly to discuss and establish enrichment programs that enable students to make the transition from school to workplace. Recent programs include instituting a career mentoring program for high-school students, conducting technology surveys, and offering students test preparation workshops. Every year the council solicits donations for scholarships given to students who plan to enter vocational fields. In the spring, the council organizes a career fair at the high school. Presenters from a variety of vocational or professional fields set up booths that the students can visit to find out more about career options. Twice a year, the council conducts mock interviews for high-school seniors. The public library provides the space for interviews, and businesspeople act as mock interviewers.

Planning Tips

Meet monthly to stay in contact, keep track of details, and provide consistent programming.

Find volunteers from a wide range of occupations.

Offer lunch before each meeting.

Meet in a central location.

Expected Outcomes

Students gain a better understanding of career opportunities.

Talented students receive scholarships to pursue education that helps them achieve their career goals.

Students receive guidance during a difficult transition period: leaving school, preparing for a career, and entering the workforce.

Community members work with each other, making use of their complementary strengths to help the next generation.

Source: Erica Christianson, Chris Franson, and the Lake Zurich High School Career Advisory Council, Lake Zurich, Illinois.

JAPANESE STORIES AND CRAFTS

Cooperating Parties

Public librarian, teacher, Japanese-speaking volunteer.

Level

Grades 1 through 5.

Program Description

The public librarian and a Japanese-speaking volunteer visit classrooms to present a story and craft. The volunteer first presents the story in Japanese while showing story cards illustrating the narrative. The students guess what the story is about based on the illustrations and the volunteer's expressions. After students finish offering possibilities, the librarian presents the story in English while showing the same illustrated story cards. The story is followed by a simple origami craft, Japanese music, and a treat: Japanese candy.

Planning Tips

Find enthusiastic volunteers through local ESL classes.

Choose an easy origami craft. Practice until the procedure becomes automatic.

Have plenty of origami paper and Japanese candy on hand.

Stock up on origami books and warn the school librarians that they may want to do the same.

Begin each presentation with an introduction to the *Kamishibai* art form. *Kamishibai* (*kami* means "paper" and *shibai* means "drama") plays were presented by men who rode bicycles through neighborhoods and sold candy. When the *Kamishibai* man was ready to tell a story, he clapped two wooden blocks together loudly. Children came running to him to buy candy and hear stories. The children who bought candy got to sit in the front rows and were able to see the pictures accompanying the story. Those who did not buy candy had to find places in the back. *Kamishibai* available today have illustrations on one side and the narrative in both English and Japanese on the other side.

Expected Outcomes

Students will be introduced to Japanese language, stories, and music.

Students and teachers will learn about *Kamishibai*, a method of Japanese storytelling that was very popular until television became widespread.

Japanese speakers learn more about the public library, the schools, and the community.

Students and teachers learn more about resources on Japanese culture available at the public library.

Resources

Kamishibai (Japanese stories in story card form) are available through

Kamishibai for Kids
P.O. Box 629
Cathedral Station
New York, NY 10025
Phone: 212-663-2471
Fax: 212-662-5836
www.kamishibai.com

The compact disk and songbook *Let's Sing! Japanese Songs for Kids in English and Japanese,* with Janet Sono and Maren Sono (1998), is also available through Kamishibai for Kids.

Lindquist, Tarry. 1997. "Bridges to Other Cultures: Infusing Cultural Studies across the Curriculum." In *Ways That Work: Putting Social Studies Standards into Practice.* Portsmouth, N.Y.: Heinemann.

Vukov, Elaine. 1997. "Kamishibai, Japanese Storytelling: The Return of an Imaginative Art." *Education about Asia* 2 (spring).

KINDERLITERARISCHE MATINÉE
(CHILDREN'S LITERATURE MORNING)

Cooperating Parties

Area librarians, teachers, and writers of children's literature.

Level

Adults.

Program Description

A well-known author of children's literature is invited to either the school or the public library for a breakfast on a weekend morning. Teachers, librarians, scholars, and others interested in children's literature meet to eat breakfast, listen to the author speak, and join in a discussion with the author and fellow participants.

Planning Tips

Establish a regular schedule for this program (such as the first Saturday in alternating months) and publish a list of the authors and the dates they will appear.

Send invitations to local teachers, librarians, and others who may be interested.

If financially possible, limit the size of the group so that people will feel they can speak and visit with the author.

Display copies of the author's books in the meeting room.

Seek out local authors who may want to become better known in their community.

If necessary, advertise the program with fliers that provide brief descriptions of the author's life and works.

Expected Outcomes

Professionals working with children's literature become acquainted with authors' lives and perspectives. As a result, they better understand and appreciate the authors' works.

Those who have attended the events can pass on stories and information about authors to students, colleagues, and library patrons.

Librarians and teachers meet others with whom they can discuss youth literature.

***

Source: International Youth Library, Munich, Germany.

LEARNING CENTERS FOR AT-RISK FIRST AND SECOND GRADERS

Cooperating Parties

Public librarians, reading teachers.

Level

Grades 1 and 2.

Program Description

This program consists of a tour of the youth services department of the public library for at-risk students, followed by activities at four learning centers and a promotion of the summer reading club. The program is aimed at students whose reading scores fall in the lowest 10 percent of their school's reading levels.

The use of learning centers enables the students to experience aspects of the library without needing advanced reading skills. The centers include an audio station, a video station, a magazine station, and a station for a read-aloud story on summer fun. The students are divided into groups and visit all stations.

Planning Tips

Prepare paper necklaces in four different colors for the students to wear. These will help each child identify which group to follow from station to station.

Adults accompanying the students should be informed, in advance, of how long the students should stay at each station.

Select a Hidden Pictures puzzle from a *Highlights* magazine and make enough copies of it for each child to have one.

Provide markers or crayons at the magazine station. Also provide a copy of a different Hidden Pictures puzzle that has already been completed so the students can see how the puzzle works.

Select three or four other magazines, such as *Ladybug* and *Your Big Backyard,* for the children to look at during their stay at the magazine section.

On one side of the summer reading club flier, describe everything in English. On the other side, translate the description into Spanish or other languages used by the students. Give the fliers to the teachers to distribute in their classrooms.

Expected Outcomes

Students who usually do not come to the library are able to experience an enjoyable tour.

Students learn that the public library has a variety of materials for readers at all levels.

Library staff observe how at-risk students respond to a variety of materials and formats.

Resources

Lobel, Arnold. 1985. *Frog and Toad Are Friends.* ("I Can Read" book and cassette.) New York: Caedmon.

Highlights, Ladybug, and *Your Big Backyard* magazines.

Source: Margaret Poska, Fremont Public Library, Mundelein, Illinois.

LIBRARIAN-TEACHER TEA

Cooperating Parties

School and public librarians, library assistants, teachers.

Level

Adults.

Program Description

The school librarian and local public librarian(s) prepare an after-school teatime for teachers. While enjoying refreshments, librarians informally ask teachers if any changes in the curriculum are coming up in the next semester or if any special projects have been planned. Teachers have the opportunity to comment on the collections and services of the public and school libraries and to request new materials for purchase.

Planning Tips

Send invitations and ask teachers to RSVP so that you know how many refreshments to prepare.

Choose special treats (carrot cake is a favorite) and present them on pretty plates.

Be prepared with pencil and paper. Although this event is very informal and people tend to just sit and chat, you will hear and overhear lots of useful information.

Bring extra posters and books to give away or exchange.

Expected Outcomes

While planning the tea, school and public librarians get to know each other better and have the chance to discuss teacher and curricular issues on an informal basis.

Teachers become more receptive to communicating with librarians.

Teachers feel appreciated when a special tea is prepared for them.

Librarians can update their collections to better meet curricular needs.

School and public librarians can discuss sharing resources.

The presence and support of a public librarian can help the school librarian feel less isolated professionally.

LIBRARY SAFARI

Cooperating Parties

Entire public library staff, school librarians, teachers of visiting grades.

Level

Grades 4 through 7.

Program Description

Classes are invited to visit the public library for tours, instruction on electronic resources, and book talks. When students arrive at the library, they are each given a Safari Observation Notebook (see figure 9.1) and pencil. Library staff members then divide the group of students into three smaller groups. One group begins their safari learning about electronic resources at the library. The second group tours the library, and the third listens to a book talk on adventure books. As the groups complete each segment, the library safari guides escort them to the location of the next segment. By the time the safari is completed, students will have attended all three segments.

A scavenger hunt is included as the fourth and final section of the Safari Observation Notebook. Students are invited to return to the library with

FIGURE 9.1
Safari Observation Notebook

OBSERVATION NOTEBOOK

name _____

school _____

SCAVENGER
HUNT

their parents, friends, or teachers to complete the scavenger hunt and put into practice the skills they learned while on the library safari. All students completing the scavenger hunt receive a prize.

Planning Tips

In the semester preceding the planned safaris, advertise the program by attending teachers' meetings and sending out informational brochures.

If your school districts are large, scheduling classes for days and times at the public library can be a nightmare. Offer teachers a set of dates and times and ask them to give you their preferred slot. If more than one person is arranging the appointments at the library, try using Yahoo! Calendar to help keep everyone up-to-date. Find it at www.calendar. yahoo.com.

Discuss transportation costs and procedures with your school districts. Transportation costs tend to discourage students and schools with less money from visiting the library. If you receive any grant money, consider using it to pay transportation costs. Decorate an area of the library as a safari cabin or hut where the students can gather and listen to the book talk. Plants, animal-print pillows, and stuffed wild animals greatly add to the atmosphere and the fun. In the background, play nature music (such as waterfall sounds, birds singing, storms).

This program is staff intensive. You will need tour guides, electronic resource instructors, and people to give book talks. Ask for volunteers from all departments and post a master schedule in the staff room listing dates and times of coming safaris accompanied by the names of individuals helping with each program.

To keep morale high, encourage those who enjoy dressing up to wear safari-related clothing. Other staff may like to help with decorations and bulletin board displays.

Expected Outcomes

Students learn fundamental research skills by exploring reference tools, the online catalog, and electronic databases.

Teachers become aware of the resources they and their students have access to at the public library.

Students apply their research skills during the scavenger hunt and obtain firsthand experience using reference books and other library resources.

Students become familiar with the layout of the public library and feel more comfortable looking for what they need.

Students realize that the public library does not cease to be fun after they grow too old for story time. The book talk emphasizes reading for recreation and the decorated safari area functions as a comfortable hang-out spot for school-age patrons.

Teachers and public librarians become further acquainted.

Students whose parents do not take them to the library are introduced to the services of a public library.

Resources

Dickinson, Peter. 1988. *Eva.* New York: Delacorte.

Fossey, Dian. 1983. *Gorillas in the Mist.* Boston: Houghton Mifflin.

George, Jean Craighead. 1996. *The Case of the Missing Cutthroats: An Ecological Mystery.* New York: HarperCollins.

Hesse, Karen. 1996. *The Music of Dolphins.* New York: Scholastic.

Hobbs, Will. 1998. *The Maze.* New York: Morrow Junior.

Paulsen, Gary. 1998. *Transall Saga.* New York: Delacorte.

Perrott, D. V. 1965. *Concise Swahili and English Dictionary.* New York: D. McKay

Rock, Maxine. 1996. *Kishina: A True Story of Gorilla Survival.* Atlanta: Peachtree.

Shusterman, Neal. 1997. *Dark Side of Nowhere: A Novel.* Boston: Little, Brown.

Springer, Nancy. 1991. *Colt.* New York: Dial.

Vande Velde, Vivian. 1998. *Smart Dog.* San Diego: Harcourt Brace.

Source: Erica Christianson and Natalie Ziarnik, Ela Area Public Library, Lake Zurich, Illinois.

LITTLE RED RIDING HOOD

Cooperating Parties

Public librarian, teachers.

Level

Grades 2 and 3.

Program Description

The public librarian visits second- and third-grade classrooms and presents different versions of the Little Red Riding Hood story. Students, teachers, and the librarian discuss the versions' similarities, differences, and possible places of origin. After the stories and discussion end, the students are given an activity sheet and some time to color the mandalas while reflecting on the fairy tale. This presentation is a nice accompaniment to curricular units on fairy tales and is often requested.

At the end of the classroom visit, the librarian encourages the students to visit the public library, where they will see a display case and bulletin board dedicated to Little Red Riding Hood. The display case houses many versions of the Little Red Riding Hood tale, which are available for checkout. The bulletin board portrays a path from Little Red Riding Hood's house through the woods to her grandmother's house. Along the path, wolves are hidden here and there. A teacher's name is written on each large tree in the forest. When students come to the public library, they each write their name on a small tree, which is then placed near their teacher's larger tree on the bulletin board.

Planning Tips

Read as many versions of the tale as possible before determining which ones to present.

If you have time, give a brief background talk on the pagan and early Christian superstitions concerning werewolves in the woods.

Discuss: What would you do if you were out in your backyard and suddenly a ferocious wolf showed up?

Ask the children what they know about meeting and talking with strangers.

Expected Outcomes

Students enjoy listening to traditional and modern versions of a popular tale.

Students learn about oral and written storytelling traditions.

Students are introduced to cultural variance in literature.

Students are introduced to archetypal patterns in literature.

Librarians learn how teachers approach the study of fairy tales.

Teachers become acquainted with fairy tale resources available at the public library.

The bulletin board display illustrates the connection between the public library and the schools.

When children see their tree next to their teacher's tree on the bulletin board, they feel part of a community that includes both school and the public library, blurring the distinctions between learning for school and learning for fun.

Children will recognize the librarian who visited the classrooms and, as a result, feel more comfortable when visiting the public library, whether for recreational or curricular materials.

Resources

Artell, Mike. 2001. *Petite Rouge: A Cajun Red Riding Hood*. Illustrated by Jim Harris. New York: Dial.

Dundes, Alan. 1989. *Little Red Riding Hood*. Madison: University of Wisconsin Press.

Rosengarten, Johannes. 2000. *Die Schönsten Märchen-Mandalas*. Würzburg, Germany: Edition Bücherbär im Arena Verlag.

Young, Ed. 1989. *Lon Po Po: A Red Riding Hood from China*. New York: Philomel.

Zipes, Jack David. 1993. *The Trials and Tribulations of Little Red Riding Hood*. New York: Routledge.

POETRY BREAK

Cooperating Parties

School librarian, public librarian, teachers, principal, other school administrators, other community members.

Level

Children and adults.

Program Description

The school librarian invites people from the community to prepare a poem to recite to the classes at school. Each participant is assigned a date and time to visit the school. On arrival at the school, he or she visits each classroom and recites a poem.

Planning Tips

Presenters should either choose a poem of interest to a wide range of ages (difficult to do) or select several poems, one for each age group.

Students enjoy simple props that accompany a poem and reinforce its meaning.

Provide signs saying "No Poetry Break" for teachers to place on their doors at times the class does not wish to be interrupted, such as during testing.

Presenters and teachers should introduce themselves to each other.

Display poetry books in the school library and at the public library.

Plan Poetry Breaks during the month of April to celebrate National Poetry Week.

Encourage students to write their own poetry and recite it to others.

Expected Outcomes

Students enjoy a spontaneous five-minute break from their daily routine.

Presenters rediscover the joy of sharing favorite poems.

Students are exposed to a wide range of poems.

Public librarians and other community members briefly meet teachers and students and become more familiar with the school environment and routine.

Resources

Bauer, Caroline Feller. 1995. *Poetry Break: An Annotated Anthology with Ideas for Introducing Children to Poetry*. Bronx, N.Y.: H. W. Wilson.

The Children's Book Council sells posters and bookmarks especially designed for National Poetry Week:

Children's Book Council
12 W. 37th Street, 2nd floor
New York, NY 10018-2160
www.cbcbooks.org

Source: Linda Fortino and Sonja Knox, Charles Quentin Elementary School, Palatine, Illinois.

PROJECT SUCCESS: SCIENCE FAIR WORKSHOP

Cooperating Parties

Public reference librarians, graphic artists.

Level

Grades 5 through 8.

Program Description

The public library offers workshops on how to choose, research, and display science fair projects. The workshop lasts forty-five minutes to one hour. Presenters use one science project topic as an example to demonstrate the research process of the scientific method.

Planning Tips

Advertise in the library's newsletter, through fliers and teacher's guides sent to area schools, and through fliers and posters in the library.

Librarians prepare and present the bibliographic part of the workshop.

The library's graphic artist prepares and presents tips on the best techniques for displaying a project.

Contact local school districts for a sample science project guide given to students.

Talk with area science fair judges or volunteer to be one yourself.

Contact local museums for more information and resources.

Expected Outcomes

Students become familiar with appropriate print and electronic resources to use for science fair projects.

Students learn the importance of library research.

Students learn how to display their projects.

Resources

Bochinski, Julianne Blair. 1996. *The Complete Handbook of Science Fair Projects.* New York: Wiley.

Brisk, Marion A. 1992. *1001 Ideas for Science Projects.* New York: Prentice Hall

Gardner, Robert. 1999. *Science Projects about Plants.* Springfield, N.J.: Enslow.

Gutnik, Martin J. 1980. *How to Do a Science Project and Report.* New York: F. Watts.

Pilger, Mary Ann E. 1996. *Science Experiments Index for Young People.* Englewood, Colo.: Libraries Unlimited.

Tocci, Salvatore. 1997. *How to Do a Science Fair Project.* New York: F. Watts.

———. 2000. *Science Fair Success in the Hardware Store.* Berkeley Heights, N.J.: Enslow.

VanCleave, Janice. 2000. *Janice VanCleave's Guide to More of the Best Science Fair Projects.* New York: Wiley.

———. 1997. *Janice VanCleave's Science Experiment Sourcebook.* New York: Wiley

Wood, Robert W. 1991. *Science for Kids: 39 Easy Astronomy Experiments.* Blue Ridge Summit, Pa.: TAB.

Web Sites

www.kids.infoplease.lycos.com/spot/sciproject1.html

www.school.discovery.com/sciencefaircentral/scifairstudio/
   handbook/presandeval.html

http://teacher.scholastic.com/products/classmags/scienceworld.htm

---

Source: Amanda Hovious, Palatine Public Library District, Palatine, Illinois.

REBECCA CAUDILL YOUNG READERS' BOOK AWARD

Cooperating Parties

School or public librarians, teachers.

Level

Grades 4 through 8.

Program Description

Schools register for the reading program and receive a packet of information including a master list of twenty selected books written by living authors. The school must make a minimum of twelve of those twenty titles available to their students. After reading or listening to at least three books on the list, each student is eligible to vote for the most outstanding book in an election in February. Voting is normally conducted by the school librarian (or a teacher if the school has no librarian). If local schools do not register for the program, the public library may sponsor the program and conduct the voting procedure. The winner is announced annually in March.

The award is named in honor of Rebecca Caudill, who lived and wrote in Urbana, Illinois, for fifty years. The award is given in recognition of her literary talent and the universal appeal of her books.

Other states have similar programs.

Planning Tips

School and public libraries should order several copies of the books on the master list. Those books are often used for book reports.

Book talks presenting the books on the master list are very effective in encouraging children and young adults to read the books, become interested in the award, and participate in the voting process.

The book talks can be given by school librarians, teachers, or public librarians.

Activities related to the award can be found on the Rebecca Caudill Web site.

The master list is an excellent starting point for recommended reading for grades 4 through 8. Titles from the list can also be incorporated into Battle of the Books lists.

Teachers are encouraged to read books from the master list aloud in their classes.

Expected Outcomes

Children and young adults read for personal satisfaction.

Librarians and teachers help develop statewide awareness of outstanding literature for children and young people.

The administration of the award program encourages cooperation among agencies providing educational and library service to young people.

Resources

Rebecca Caudill Web site: www.rebeccacaudill.org.

Video: *Child of Appalachia: Rebecca Caudill Talks about Her Life and Her Writing.* Available for $60 from

> Child of Appalachia Video
> Division of Media Services
> Northern Illinois University
> DeKalb, IL 60115-2854

Students may submit pictures or reviews of the nominated books to the official Rebecca Caudill Web site by writing Penny Mandziara at Bensenville Community Public Library, 200 S. Church Road, Bensenville, IL 60106.

Source: Illinois Reading Council, Illinois Association of Teachers of English, and the Illinois School Library Media Association, Rebecca Caudill Committee.

STUDENT STORYTELLERS

Cooperating Parties

Public librarians, middle- and elementary-school teachers, graphic artist.

Level

Storytellers are in middle school; audience consists of students in grades K through 3 and their families.

Program Description

The middle-school students choose a book to read aloud to the elementary-school students in their district. The presenters enhance their stories with props, posters, costumes, flannel board pieces, group repetition of action rhymes, and other cooperative activities. Presentations are made in pairs, with one storyteller and one helper. The middle-school students travel by bus from their school to the three elementary schools. Costs may be covered by a grant. (For example, costs in the Fremont Public Library District are covered by a grant from the Mundelein Educational Foundation.)

The public library becomes involved from the very beginning of the assignment when the middle-school teachers call to give the librarians a list of appropriate stories and ask for other recommended titles. The librarians prepare a cart of books that fit the teachers' requirements. Students are directed to the cart when they visit the library.

After presenting the stories in the schools, the middle-school students prepare for an evening performance open to all at the public library.

Planning Tips

Ask your graphics department to create fliers advertising the program as well as certificates for the storytellers.

Prepare a list or chart for the teachers to fill out that will designate the names of students performing. Fax or mail this list to the school about three weeks before the program date. Include photo release forms for the students' parents to sign.

Send a press release to the local newspapers about two weeks before the program.

Invite the middle-school principal and participating teachers to the evening performance.

Save newspaper clippings featuring the event.

Expected Outcomes

The student storytellers develop increased confidence in public speaking. Middle-school students have a positive experience in the public library.

Resources

Carle, Eric. 1984. *The Very Busy Spider.* New York: Philomel.

Lester, Helen. 1987. *Pookins Gets Her Way.* Boston: Houghton Mifflin.

———. 1986. *A Porcupine Named Fluffy.* Boston: Houghton Mifflin.

Munsch, Robert. 1986. *50 below Zero.* Toronto, Canada: Annick.

Oppenheim, Joanne. 1989. *"Not Now!" Said the Cow.* New York: Bantam.

Ross, Tom. 1994. *Eggbert, the Slightly Cracked Egg.* New York: Putnam.

Seuss, Dr. 1990. *Oh, the Places You'll Go.* New York: Random House.

Slobodkina, Esphyr. 1947. *Caps for Sale.* New York: Harper and Row.

Stevens, Janet. 1999. *Cook-a-Doodle-Doo.* San Diego: Harcourt Brace.

Source: Margaret Poska, Fremont Public Library District, Mundelein, Illinois.

SUMMER READING PROMOTION SKIT

Cooperating Parties

Public librarians, school librarians, principals.

Level

Grades K through 5.

Program Description

Public librarians write and prepare a skit to be performed in the schools. This skit is generally very humorous and encourages students to register for the summer reading program at the public library. At the end of the skit, librarians pass out materials describing the details of the summer reading program.

Planning Tips

Begin writing and preparing the skit early, in late winter.

Schedule visits to the schools early as well. Talk with the principal instead of with individual teachers. The visits should occur in May, just before the beginning of the public library's reading program.

When possible, present the skit to each school only once. The students can gather in the cafeteria or gymnasium as a large assembly.

Carefully select props and costumes that are not too cumbersome to transport from the library to the school.

Videotape the skit. Classes that may have missed the live performance can borrow the video and receive the same information.

Expected Outcomes

Student participation in summer reading dramatically increases.

Teachers become familiar with the public library's program and encourage their students to participate.

Students come to recognize the public librarians presenting the skit and feel more comfortable approaching them at the public library.

Details of the summer reading program become familiar to students, leading to smoother administration of the program.

———————

Source: Carmel Clay Public Library, Carmel, Indiana.

WHAT A WONDERFUL WORLD

Cooperating Parties

Public librarian, teachers.

Level

This multicultural program can be adapted for children in grades K through 5. The description and list of resources below have worked especially well for first graders.

Program Description

At the beginning of the fall semester, the public library sends out postcards reminding first-grade teachers to schedule a class visit to the library. Classes come to the public library with their teachers for one hour for multicultural stories, music, videos, and crafts.

Planning Tips

Read only a couple of books; show pictures from the other titles to encourage the children to check out the books and discover what it's like to grow up in a different culture or country.

Try telling *Mama Provi and the Pot of Rice,* by Sylvia Rosa-Casanova, as an active story with props.

While playing the song "What a Wonderful World" by Louis Armstrong, show pictures in the book of the same title illustrated by Weiss.

For a craft, prepare face shapes in a variety of skin colors. The children can draw and color the shapes to create multicultural faces.

The children can also make string-a-long people, all holding hands. Provide materials so the children can dress and decorate the people to represent different cultural traditions.

Expected Outcomes

Children accept and enjoy different cultures and traditions at an early age.

Children and their teachers become familiar with their public library and the resources available there.

Children's enjoyment of color and art develops into deeper appreciation of racial differences and of the strength and beauty of diversity.

Resources

Ajmera, Maya. 1997. *Children from Australia to Zimbabwe: A Photographic Journey around the World.* Watertown, Mass.: Charlesbridge.

———. 1999. *To Be a Kid.* Watertown, Mass.: Charlesbridge.

Armstrong, Louis. 1988. *What a Wonderful World*. New York: Bluebird/RCA.

Fox, Mem. 1997. *Whoever You Are*. San Diego: Harcourt Brace.

Frank, Marjorie. 1976. *I Can Make a Rainbow: Things to Create and Do, for Children and Their Grown-up Friends*. Nashville, Tenn.: Incentive.

Hamanaka, Sheila. 1994. *All the Colors of the Earth*. New York: Morrow.

Igus, Toyomi. 1996. *Two Mrs. Gibsons*. San Francisco: Children's Book Press.

Intrater. Roberta Grobel. 1995. *Two Eyes, a Nose, and a Mouth*. New York: Cartwheel.

Katz, Karen. 1999. *The Colors of Us*. New York: Holt.

Kindersley, Anabel. 1997. *Celebrations*. New York: DK.

Nikola-Lisa, W. 1994. *Bein' with You This Way*. New York: Lee and Low.

Weiss, George. 1995. *What a Wonderful World*. New York: Atheneum.

Book Prop: *Mama Provi and the Pot of Rice*. Available from

Book Props, LLC
1120 McVey Avenue
Lake Oswego, OR 97034
Phone: 800-636-5314
Fax: 503-636-8724
www.bookprops.com
sales@bookprops.com

Source: Judy Salganik, Rolling Meadows Public Library, Rolling Meadows, Illinois.

References

Ajmera, Maya. 1997. *Children from Australia to Zimbabwe: A Photographic Journey around the World*. Watertown, Mass.: Charlesbridge.

———. 1999. *To Be a Kid*. Watertown, Mass.: Charlesbridge.

Anderson, Dorothy J. 1981. Mildred L. Batchelder: A Study in Leadership. Ph.D. diss., Texas Woman's University.

Armstrong, Louis. 1988. *What a Wonderful World*. New York: Bluebird/RCA.

Artell, Mike. 2001. *Petite Rouge: A Cajun Red Riding Hood*. Illustrated by Jim Harris. New York: Dial.

Barron, Daniel D. 1995. "School Library Media Program Women: A Celebration of Our Female Heritage." *School Library Media Activities Monthly* 11, no. 7 (March).

Bauer, Caroline Feller. 1995. *Poetry Break: An Annotated Anthology with Ideas for Introducing Children to Poetry*. Bronx, N.Y.: H. W. Wilson.

Bauer, David G. 1999. *The "How-to" Grants Manual*. Rev. ed. Westport, Conn.: Greenwood.

Bochinski, Julianne Blair. 1996. *The Complete Handbook of Science Fair Projects*. New York: Wiley.

Brisk, Marion A. 1992. *1,001 Ideas for Science Projects*. New York: Prentice Hall.

Cantarella, Gina-Marie, and Foundation Center. 1999. *National Guide to Funding for Elementary and Secondary Education*. 5th ed. New York: Foundation Center.

Carle, Eric. 1984. *The Very Busy Spider*. New York: Philomel.

Cook, Sybilla, Frances Corcoran, and Beverley Fonnesbeck. 2001. *Battle of the Books and More: Reading Activities for Middle School Students*. Fort Atkinson, Wis.: Alleyside.

Dickinson, Peter. 1988. *Eva*. New York: Delacorte.

Dundes, Alan. 1989. *Little Red Riding Hood*. Madison: University of Wisconsin Press.

Edwards, Margaret A. 1969. *The Fair Garden and the Swarm of Beasts: The Library and the Young Adult*. New York: Hawthorn.

Fitzgibbons, Shirley A. 2001. "School and Public Library Relationships: Déjà vu or New Beginnings." *Journal of Youth Services in Libraries* 14, no. 3 (spring): 3–7.

Fossey, Dian. 1983. *Gorillas in the Mist*. Boston: Houghton Mifflin.

Foundation Center Staff, Gina-Marie Cantarella, eds. *2001 National Guide to Funding for Libraries and Information Services*. 6th ed. New York: Foundation Center.

Fox, Mem. 1997. *Whoever You Are*. San Diego: Harcourt Brace.

Frank, Marjorie. 1976. *I Can Make a Rainbow: Things to Create and Do, for Children and Their Grown-up Friends*. Nashville, Tenn.: Incentive.

Gardner, Robert. 1999. *Science Projects about Plants*. Springfield, N.J.: Enslow.

George, Jean Craighead. 1996. *The Case of the Missing Cutthroats: An Ecological Mystery*. New York: HarperCollins.

Gibbons, Gail. 1993. *Frogs*. New York: Holiday House.

Grassian, Esther S., and Joan R. Kaplowitz. 2001. *Information Literacy Instruction: Theory and Practice*. New York: Neal-Schuman.

Gutnik, Martin J. 1980. *How to Do a Science Project and Report*. New York: F. Watts.

Hamanaka, Sheila. 1994. *All the Colors of the Earth*. New York: Morrow.

Harshman, Marc. 1999. *All the Way to Morning*. New York: Marshall Cavendish.

Henne, Frances. 1966. "Learning to Learn in School Libraries." *School Libraries* 15, no. 4 (May).

Hesse, Karen. 1996. *The Music of Dolphins.* New York: Scholastic.

Hobbs, Will. 1998. *The Maze.* New York: Morrow Junior.

Hoffman, Mary. 1991. *Amazing Grace.* New York: Dial.

Igus, Toyomi. 1996. *Two Mrs. Gibsons.* San Francisco: Children's Book Press.

Intrater, Roberta Grobel. 1995. *Two Eyes, a Nose, and a Mouth.* New York: Cartwheel.

Jenkins, Christine. 1996. "Professional Jurisdiction and ALA Youth Services Women: Of Nightingales, Newberies, Realism, and the Right Books, 1937–1945." *Library Trends* 44, no. 4 (spring): 683–718.

———. 1995. The Strength of the Inconspicuous: Youth Services Librarians, the American Library Association, and Intellectual Freedom for the Young, 1939–1955. Ph.D. diss., University of Wisconsin–Madison.

Katz, Karen. 1999. *The Colors of Us.* New York: Holt.

Kindersley, Anabel. 1997. *Celebrations.* New York: DK.

Konigsburg, E. L. 1967. *From the Mixed-up Files of Mrs. Basil E. Frankweiler.* New York: Atheneum.

Krashen, Stephen. 1993. *The Power of Reading: Insights from the Research.* Englewood, Colo.: Libraries Unlimited.

Lester, Helen. 1987. *Pookins Gets Her Way.* Boston: Houghton Mifflin.

———. 1986. *A Porcupine Named Fluffy.* Boston: Houghton Mifflin.

Lindquist, Tarry. 1997. "Bridges to Other Cultures: Infusing Cultural Studies across the Curriculum." *Ways That Work: Putting Social Studies Standards into Practice.* Portsmouth, N.Y.: Heinemann.

Lobel, Arnold. 1970. *Frog and Toad Are Friends.* New York: Harper and Row.

———. 1985. *Frog and Toad Are Friends.* ("I Can Read" book and cassette.) New York: Caedmon.

Lowry, Lois. 1993. *The Giver.* Boston: Houghton Mifflin.

Lundin, Anne. 1996. "The Pedagogical Context of Women in Children's Services and Literature Scholarship." *Library Trends* 44, no. 4 (spring): 683–718.

Marcus, Leonard S. 1992. *Margaret Wise Brown: Awakened by the Moon.* Boston: Beacon.

Mediavilla, Cindy. 2001. *Creating the Full-Service Homework Center in Your Library.* Chicago: American Library Association.

Moore, Anne Carroll. 1902. "Library Visits to Public Schools." *Library Journal* 27 (April).

Munsch, Robert N. 1986. *50 below Zero.* Toronto, Canada: Annick.

New, Cheryl Carter, and James Aaron Quick. 1998. *Grantseeker's Toolkit.* New York: Wiley.

Nikola-Lisa, W. 1994. *Bein' with You This Way.* New York: Lee and Low.

Nixon, Joan Lowery. 1985. *The House on Hackman's Hill.* New York: Scholastic.

Nottingham, Stephen. 1998. *Eat Your Genes: How Genetically Modified Food Is Entering Our Diet.* Cape Town: University of Cape Town Press.

Oppenheim, Joanne. 1989. *"Not now!" Said the Cow.* New York: Bantam.

Park, Linda Sue. 2001. *A Single Shard.* New York: Clarion.

Paulsen, Gary. 1998. *The Transall Saga.* New York: Delacorte.

Pawley, Christine. 2000. "Advocate for Access: Lutie Stearns and the Traveling Libraries of the Wisconsin Free Library Commission, 1895–1914." *Libraries and Culture* 35, no. 3 (summer).

Perrott, D. V. 1965. *Concise Swahili and English Dictionary.* New York: D. McKay.

Pilger, Mary Anne. 1996. *Science Experiments Index for Young People.* Englewood, Colo.: Libraries Unlimited, 1996.

Pond, Patricia. 1982. The American Association for School Librarians, 1896–1951. Ph.D. diss., University of Chicago.

Rock, Maxine A. 1996. *Kishina: The True Story of Gorilla Survival.* Atlanta: Peachtree.

Rockfield, Gary. 1998. "Beyond Library Power: Reader's Digest Adds Public Libraries to the Mix." *School Library Journal* (January): 30–33.

Rosa-Casanova, Sylvia. 1997. *Mama Provi and the Pot of Rice.* New York: Atheneum.

Rosengarten, Johannes. 2000. *Die Schönsten Märchen-Mandalas.* Würzburg, Germany: Edition Bücherbär im Arena Verlag.

Ross, Tom. 1994. *Eggbert, the Slightly Cracked Egg.* New York: Putnam.

Sager, Don. 1997. "Beating the Homework Blues." *Public Libraries* (January/February): 19–23.

Sayers, Frances Clarke. 1972. *Anne Carroll Moore.* New York: Antheneum.

Schneider, Dorothy, and Carl J. Schneider. 1993. *American Women in the Progressive Era.* New York: Facts on File.

Seuss, Dr. 1990. *Oh, the Places You'll Go!* New York: Random House.

Shusterman, Neal. 1997. *The Dark Side of Nowhere: A Novel.* Boston: Little, Brown.

Slobodkina, Esphyr. 1947. *Caps for Sale.* New York: Harper and Row.

Sono, Janet, and Maren Sono. 1998. *Let's Sing! Japanese Songs for Kids in English and Japanese.* New York: Kamishibai for Kids.

Springer, Nancy. 1991. *Colt.* New York: Dial.

Stevens, Janet. 1999. *Cook-a-Doodle-Doo!* San Diego: Harcourt Brace.

Taft Group for the American Library Association. 2002. *The Big Book of Library Grant Money 2002–2003.* Chicago: American Library Association.

Tarin, Patricia A., and Barbara Turnbull. 2001. *Tall Tree: Sharing the Vision: How Schools and Libraries Can Work Together to Serve Children Better.* 3 vols. Pleasantville, N.Y.: Reader's Digest Foundation.

Tocci, Salvatore. 1997. *How to Do a Science Fair Project.* New York: F. Watts.

———. 2000. *Science Fair Success in the Hardware Store.* Berkeley Heights, N.J.: Enslow.

Utz, Lois. 1968. *The Pineapple Duck with the Peppermint Bill.* Indianapolis: Bobbs-Merrill.

VanCleave, Janice. 2000. *Janice VanCleave's Guide to More of the Best Science Fair Projects.* New York: Wiley.

———. 1997. *Janice VanCleave's Science Experiment Sourcebook.* New York: Wiley.

Vande Velde, Vivian. 1998. *Smart Dog.* San Diego: Harcourt Brace.

Vukov, Elaine. 1997. "Kamishibai, Japanese Storytelling: The Return of An Imaginative Art." *Education about Asia* 2 (spring).

Weiss, George. 1995. *What a Wonderful World*. New York: Atheneum.

Wood, Robert W. 1991. *Science for Kids: 39 Easy Astronomy Experiments.* Blue Ridge Summit, Pa.: TAB.

Yolen, Jane. 1987. *Owl Moon*. New York: Philomel.

Young, Ed. 1989. *Lon Po Po: A Red Riding Hood from China*. New York: Philomel.

Zipes, Jack David. 1993. *The Trials and Tribulations of Little Red Riding Hood*. New York: Routledge.

Index